25 BICYCLE TOURS
in Maryland

Other Books by Anne H. Oman

25 Bicycle Tours in and around Washington, D.C.
(Backcountry Publications)

Saturday's Child: Family Activities in Metropolitan Washington
(Washington Book Trading Company)

25

BICYCLE TOURS
in Maryland

*from the Allegheny Mountains
to the Atlantic Ocean*

Anne H. Oman

photographs by the author

Backcountry Publications
Woodstock · Vermont

An invitation to the reader

Although it is unlikely that the roads you cycle on these tours will change much with time, some road signs, landmarks, and other items may. If you find that such changes have occurred on these routes, please let the author and publisher know, so that corrections may be made in future editions. Other comments and suggestions are also welcome. Address all correspondence to:

Editor, 25 Bicycle Tours™ Series
Backcountry Publications
P.O. Box 748
Woodstock, Vermont 05091

Library of Congress Cataloging-in-Publication Data

Oman, Anne H.
    25 bicycle tours in Maryland : from the Allegheny Mountains to the Atlantic Ocean / by Anne Oman.
       p.   cm.
    ISBN 0-88150-287-1
    1. Bicycle touring—Maryland—Guidebooks.   2. Bicycle trails—Maryland—Guidebooks.   3. Maryland—Guidebooks.
I. Title.   II. Title: Twenty-five bicycle tours in Maryland.
GV1045.5.M3043   1994
796.6'4'09752—dc20   93–45462
                       CIP

Second Printing 1996

Book design by Sally Sherman
Cover and interior photographs by Anne H. Oman
Maps by Dick Widhu, © 1994 The Countryman Press

Published by Backcountry Publications, A division of The Countryman Press, Woodstock, VT 05091

Distributed by W.W. Norton & Company, Inc., 500 Fifth Avenue, New York, NY 10110

Printed in the United States of America
10 9 8 7 6 5 4 3 2

Acknowledgments

I'd like to thank the following people who rode with me in a dauntless quest for truth, or at least, accuracy: Ralph Oman, Tabitha Oman, Caroline Oman, Charlotte Oman, Dwayne Poston, Nancy Martin, Summer Martin, Diana Cadeddu, Mark Joelson, Tato Joelson, Charlie Borden, Tina Borden, Gary Ferraro, Kathryn Ferraro, Joslin Frank, Matt Erskine, Ann Webber, Mike Remington, Elise Remington, Christophe Remington, Lorna Ferguson, and Terry Clark.

Publisher's notice

Cycling involves inherent risks, and readers planning to follow tours in this book should first read carefully the "safety" section of the introduction. Cyclists in urban areas should also be alert to the problem of crime. Tours in this book are in areas considered safe to ride in at the time of publication, but cyclists should follow sensible precautions (such as never cycling at night and traveling with one or more companions) and should be alert to changing patterns of crime in the city.

*This book is dedicated, with love and gratitude,
to Ralph Oman,
who fixed flats, loaded the bike rack, read maps,
and did on-the-spot repairs.*

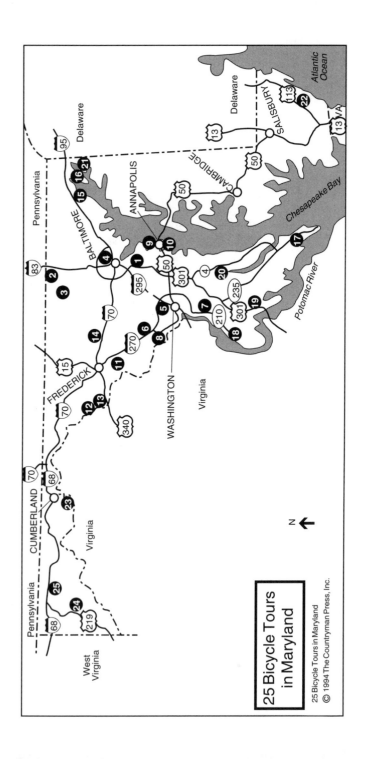

25 Bicycle Tours
in Maryland

25 Bicycle Tours in Maryland
© 1994 The Countryman Press, Inc.

Contents

Introduction

Maryland's almost 10,000 square miles encompass incredibly varied terrain, from the almost flat coastal plain, to the foothills of the Piedmont, to the Appalachians, with elevations of more than 3,000 feet. To the cyclist, this offers a wide choice of rides—from effortless glides through the farmland of the Eastern Shore to challenging assaults on the western hills, with myriad options in between.

The state also has a long and colorful history, which can be experienced in visits to Native American longhouses, to archaeological digs of the first European settlements, to graves of Revolutionary War soldiers, to forts used in the War of 1812, to Civil War battlefields, to early industrial sites, to twentieth-century cities and suburbs, and to places where the timeless rhythm of agricultural pursuits still rules.

This book attempts to allow the cyclist to sample the land and history of Maryland from the seat of a bicycle.

About the Rides

The tours in this book vary not only in terrain, but in length—from five to 95 miles. Some use off-road trails, shared with hikers and horses, while others use roads shared with cars. Trails and light-traffic roads are to be preferred, especially if you have children in your party. An attempt has been made to avoid roads with heavy traffic, but this was impossible in a few cases.

Because different cyclists set different paces, I haven't tried to estimate the time necessary to complete a tour. Even inexperienced cyclists can usually average about 12 miles per hour while actually cycling, but if you like to stop often to rest, eat, or sightsee, the hourly average will drop to about five miles. By that rule of thumb, a 40-mile trip will take about eight hours. For some tours, accommodations along the route are listed.

The tours are organized according to their proximity to four cities—Baltimore; Washington, DC; Annapolis; and Frederick—and, other-

The dunes of Assateague Island, on the Atlantic, form Maryland's easternmost boundary.

wise, according to broad geographical areas: the Eastern Shore, Southern Maryland, Northeast Maryland, and Western Maryland.

Rules of the Road

Bicycles are prohibited on expressways and other controlled-access highways as well as toll facilities such as bridges and tunnels. On other highways where the posted speed is more than 50 miles per hour, bicycles are banned from the travel lanes and must ride on the shoulder, even if the shoulder is unpaved. Along any other highways, cyclists must use the shoulder or bike lane if it is paved.

On all roads where bicycling is allowed, the operator must
- obey all traffic signals and signs;
- ride with the traffic as near to the right of the road or shoulder as possible;

- use standard hand signals;
- yield to pedestrians;
- move to the right or stop for emergency vehicles;
- stop for loading and unloading of schoolbuses when warning lights are flashing;
- obey all applicable traffic laws, such as the one prohibiting passing on the right.

Bicycles must be equipped with
- brakes that make the braked wheel skid on dry, clean pavement;
- a bell or horn;
- a rear red reflector;
- a white-beam headlight (if ridden at night).

In addition, the Maryland Department of Transportation strongly encourages the use of a bicycle helmet, rearview mirror, and red taillight.

Resources

The Maryland State Highway Administration has a Bicycle Affairs Coordinator, who performs research and monitors state highway projects for bicycle compatibility. This office offers a number of free brochures on bicycle safety, regulations, ferry service, and trails. For information, write to: Bicycle Affairs Coordinator, Room 218, Maryland State Highway Administration, 707 North Calvert Street, Baltimore, MD 21202, 1-800-252-8776.

The state also operates a bicycle information hotline, which is staffed from 8:30 AM to 4:30 PM weekdays: 1-800-252-8776. By calling this number and leaving your name and mailing address, you can also request a packet of free bicycling information.

The Department of Economic and Employment Development has published a color-coded "Maryland Bicycle Touring Map." It is available free from the Office of Tourism Development, 217 East Redwood Street, Baltimore, MD 21202, 1-800-543-1036.

About Safety

Cycling involves two kinds of safety considerations—safety from possible criminal activity as well as from traffic hazards. The tours in this book are all in areas considered safe, in daylight hours, at the time of publication. But "safe" is a relative term, and no place is completely without danger. Prudent cyclists will use common sense to protect themselves and their bikes against crime and other dangers. In addition to following the state laws concerning cycling (see "Rules of the Road" above), the following guidelines should be used.

- Never ride alone, particularly on a secluded trail or road.
- Always let someone know what route you are taking.
- Don't ride after dark.
- Carry a whistle around your neck or an air horn in an accessible pocket. Noise can both bring help and scare away attackers.
- When riding with companions, ride single file at least 20 feet apart.
- Don't wear headsets or earplugs.
- Be sure your bicycle is in good working order.
- Watch out for storm drains, potholes, railroad or trolley tracks, patches of sand or gravel, and other road hazards.
- Ride defensively. Expect the unexpected—such as someone opening a car door on your side.
- Pull well away from the road when you stop to rest or check the map.

Bike Security

Always secure your bike when you leave it—even for a few minutes. This is especially important in urban areas, where bicycle theft is a serious problem. The kind of lock most likely to foil bicycle thieves is the U-shaped shackle lock, sold under such brand names as Kryptonite and Citadel. These are expensive, but not as expensive as a new bicycle. And police departments in some jurisdictions report that bicycle thefts

Baltimore's Inner Harbor attracts visitors with its shops, restaurants, museums, and ships.

have actually declined since these locks were introduced in the 1970s. Here are some additional security tips:

- Lock your bike to something permanent and in a place where any attempted theft is likely to be noticed.
- Lock up as much of your bike as possible. If you have quick-release wheels, remove the front wheel and put the lock through the front wheel, the rear wheel, and the frame, securing it to the rack, tree, or other fixture. Remove any accessories you don't want to lose—pumps, water bottles, and computer-type odometers are vulnerable to theft.
- Register your bike with the local police department. This will greatly enhance your chances of getting it back if it's stolen.

About Equipment

In addition to the equipment required or recommended by the Maryland Department of Transportation (see "Rules of the Road" above), you should carry a patch kit, a spare tube, and an air pump. An odometer is handy for gauging distance, although you should be able to follow the directions in this book without one.

Rentals

Many bicycle shops rent bikes, racks, child carriers, helmets, and other equipment. At the end of each tour in this book, at least one bicycle shop is listed. Those that rent bikes are indicated. It's best to reserve the equipment you want in advance.

About Metrorail

Two of the tours in this book (tour 6, "So We Beat On. . ." and tour 9, "Capital-to-Capital Express") suggest using Metrorail as an alternative way of getting to and from the starting point. The Washington Metropolitan Area Transit Authority allows bicyclists with permits to bring their bikes on the trains after 7:00 PM and on weekends and holidays except July 4. To obtain a permit you must appear in person at the Metro headquarters at 600 Fifth Street NW, Washington, DC, for a briefing and test on the common-sense bike-on-rail rules. Permits are good for three years, and a fee is charged. Call 202-962-1116 for more information and for the hours when permits are issued. If you don't want to use Metrorail, the stations used as starting points in the tours involved have parking lots, which are free on weekends.

Bicycle Clubs

The Maryland Department of Transportation lists the following recreational cycling clubs:

Annapolis Bicycle Club
P.O. Box 224, Annapolis, MD 21404

Appalachian Bicycle Club
P.O. Box 1254, Cumberland, MD 21502

Baltimore Bicycling Club
P.O. Box 5906, Baltimore, MD 21208

Cumberland Valley Cycling Club
P.O. Box 711, Hagerstown, MD 21740

Frederick Peddlars
P.O. Box 1293 Frederick, MD 21701

Freestate Derailleurs
4424 MacWorth Place, Baltimore, MD 21236

Oxon Hill Bicycle and Trail Club
P.O. Box 81, Oxon Hill, MD 20745

Patuxent Area Cycling Enthusiasts
P.O. Box 1318, Solomons, MD 20688

Potomac Pedalers Touring Club
P.O. Box 23601, L'Enfant Plaza Station, Washington, DC 20026

Salisbury Bicycle Club
708 Walnut Street, Pocomoke City, MD 21851

Cycle Across Maryland (CAM)

Every summer, usually toward the end of July, hundreds of cycling enthusiasts of widely varying abilities pedal across the state, or a good part of it. The route changes from year to year, and the trip usually takes four or five days. Participants pay a fee and stay at campgrounds, in facilities such as schools, or in motels and guesthouses. The event is widely publicized through bicycle shops and newspapers, and the state Bicycle Coordinator can also provide information.

GREATER
BALTIMORE

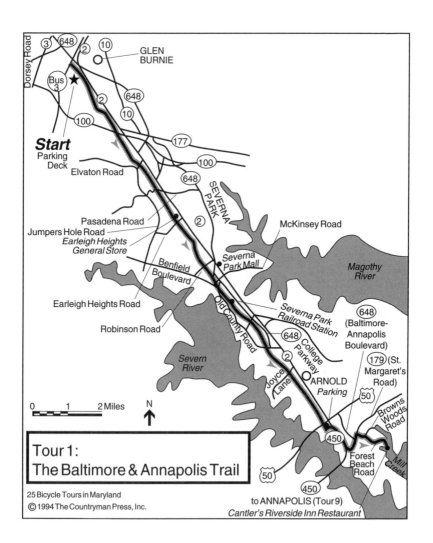

Tour 1:
The Baltimore & Annapolis Trail

25 Bicycle Tours in Maryland
© 1994 The Countryman Press, Inc.

1
The Baltimore & Annapolis Trail

Location: Anne Arundel County
Terrain: Flat on bike trail, some hills on extension
Road conditions: Paved trail and paved roads
Distance: 13.3 miles on the trail, 18.5 miles if you continue to the restaurant
Highlights: Woods, wetlands, the Earleigh Heights General Store, the Severna Park Railroad Station, Cantler's Riverside Inn Restaurant

The Baltimore & Annapolis Trail Park, associated with the Rails to Trails Conservancy, follows the track bed of the defunct Baltimore & Annapolis Railroad from its northern terminus in Glen Burnie, a Baltimore suburb, to Annapolis, Maryland's seagoing capital. The 10-foot-wide path traverses a variety of landscapes—exurban shopping malls, small cities, backyards, and wildlife habitats. The trail ends across the Severn River from historic Annapolis, but the tour continues on country and suburban roads to a popular crab house on Mill Creek. The trail begins in Glen Burnie, on Dorsey Road just east of MD 3, and there is a parking lot.

0.0   From the parking lot, head south on the trail.

0.5   The trail leads through downtown Glen Burnie and crosses MD 3.

3.0   After crossing MD 100 on a bridge, the trail winds downhill.

4.3   At the intersection with Jumpers Hole Road are picnic tables, a gazebo, and a food store.

4.6 *The trail runs through a wetland, then into some woods replete with wild dogwood and ferns.*

6.3 *The Earleigh Heights General Store, c. 1890, now houses an information center and rest rooms.*

A liquor store across the trail sells sodas and snacks.

9.0 *The restored Severna Park Railroad Station was built in 1919.*

In an exhibit case is a picture of the last train to run on this line, in 1950. In the surrounding center of this upscale suburb are an antique shop and a shopping mall with an ice cream store.

10.3 *The final stretch of the trail passes through suburban Arnold's heavily shaded backyards.*

13.3 *After crossing under US 50, the off-road trail ends. Continue on a marked side-of-the-road path along Boulter's Way to the parking lot, which is at the intersection with MD 450.*

14.0 *If you want to continue the tour, turn right on MD 450 from the parking lot and ride on the paved shoulder.*

15.6 *Cross the highway—carefully—and climb some steps to a scenic overlook with a view of the Naval Academy, the Statehouse, and Annapolis Harbor.*

15.9 *At the light, MD 450 crosses the Severn into downtown Annapolis (see tour 9). This tour turns left on Baltimore-Annapolis Boulevard (MD 648) and travels through a posh residential section.*

17.0 *Turn right on St. Margaret's Road (MD 179).*

17.3 *At the fork marked by Sandy's Country Store, bear right on Brown's Wood Road, which climbs a small hill.*

17.5 *Turn right on Forest Beach Road.*

18.5 *The road dead-ends at Cantler's Riverside Inn Restaurant,*

Cyclists pedal the trail in the roadbed of the railroad
that once linked Baltimore and Annapolis.

*where you can end your trip with excellent crabs or other food
and a view of Mill Creek.*

Bicycle Repair Services

Bike Doctor, Inc.
953 Ritchie Highway, Arnold
410-544-3532
No rentals

The Bike Peddlars
5 Central Avenue, Glen Burnie
410-761-7675
Rentals

Pete's Cycle Company, Inc.
800 Ritchie Highway, Severna Park
410-647-8292
No rentals

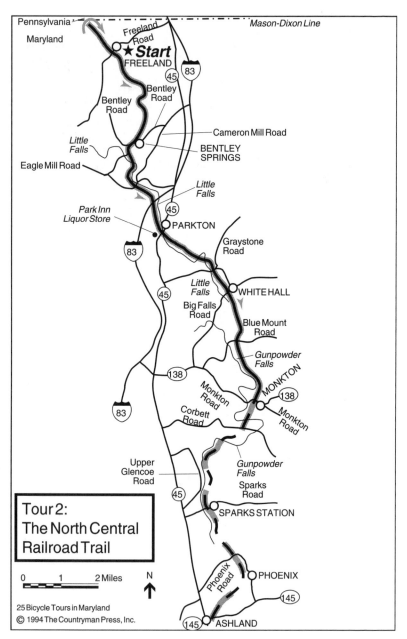

Pennsylvania

Maryland

Mason-Dixon Line

Freeland Road

★ *Start*
FREELAND

45 83

Bentley Road

Bentley Road

Cameron Mill Road

Little Falls

BENTLEY SPRINGS

Eagle Mill Road

Little Falls

45

Park Inn Liquor Store

83

PARKTON

Graystone Road

Little Falls

45

WHITE HALL

Big Falls Road

Blue Mount Road

Gunpowder Falls

138

Monkton Road

MONKTON

138

Monkton Road

83

Corbett Road

Upper Glencoe Road

45

Gunpowder Falls

Sparks Road

SPARKS STATION

Phoenix Road

PHOENIX

145

145 ASHLAND

Tour 2:
The North Central
Railroad Trail

0   1   2 Miles   N

25 Bicycle Tours in Maryland
© 1994 The Countryman Press, Inc.

24

2

North Central Railroad Trail

Location: *Baltimore County*
Terrain: *Flat*
Road conditions: *Crushed-stone hiker-biker trail*
Distance: *14.6 miles (or 21.7 miles)*
Highlights: *Picturesque small towns and farms, Little Falls, the Gunpowder River, the Monkton railroad station*

To deliver his address at the site of the battle of Gettysburg, Lincoln traveled on the North Central Railroad; after his assassination, his body was taken west along these same tracks. Union soldiers were also transported on this line. Built in 1838 to carry flour, paper, milk, farm products, coal, and mail between such settlements as White Hall, Parkton, and Bentley Springs and the city of Baltimore, the North Central gradually gave way to truck transport. In 1972 Hurricane Agnes delivered the death blow, washing out bridges. In 1984 the tracks were removed and replaced by a recreational-use trail.

The trail extends from Ashland north to the Pennsylvania state line. This tour covers the northern two-thirds of the trail, which is pretty and not heavily traveled. It begins at the Freeland parking lot (two miles west of MD 45 on Freeland Road), takes a short detour to the north end of the trail at the Mason-Dixon Line, then travels down the trail to the preserved turn-of-the-century railroad station at Monkton.

0.0 *From the Freeland parking lot, turn left past the rest rooms and follow the trail north, up a slight grade, past farmhouses and through woods.*

Watch for horse piles and hikers as this is a multi-use trail.

1.5 *The trail ends at the Pennsylvania border, or Mason-Dixon Line.*

Plans to extend the trail into Pennsylvania are awaiting funding. The trip back down the trail affords a pleasant downhill glide. Return to the Freeland parking lot.

3.0 *Across a stream from the Freeland parking lot (right), the Flower Cafe sells snacks and shaved ice.*

Chairs and tables along the stream offer a respite. Continuing south on the trail, you'll pass Victorian homes with rocking chairs, which once afforded residents a view of the passing trains.

3.2 *As you cross the stream, look at the remains of the railroad tracks to your right.*

This part of the trail winds through woods. Roads cross at intervals, so observe stop signs.

6.3 *The trail crosses Little Falls, which is not actually a falls but a popular canoeing river.*

8.7 *The brick building to your left, now a private home, was once an inn for travelers. For refreshments, turn right for 0.1 mile, following the sign that advertises "pit beef."*

On weekends, a family sells barbecued beef in front of the Park Inn liquor store. Soda machines are available when the liquor store is closed, on Sundays.

8.9 *After this detour, turn right and continue south on the trail.*

Paths through the woods lead down to Little Falls, whose waters form inviting pools around boulders. Ferns line the banks of both stream and trail, creating a green glade.

11.0 *An antique store to your left lures cyclists from the trail in the village of White Hall.*

Cows and horses graze in the field next to the store.

The restored Monkton station on the North Central Railroad Trail
houses a small museum about the railroad.

11.1 **The neoclassical White Hall National Bank dates from 1909.**

Just past White Hall, the trail runs along Gunpowder Falls, a popular tubing course.

14.6 **The Monkton Railroad Station, c. 1898, now houses a small museum and shop.**

Restrooms are available here. Across the parking lot, which gets crowded on weekends, the Monkton General Store sells sandwiches, drinks, and shave ice. Additional parking lots south of Monkton are at Sparks (on Sparks Road east from MD 45), at Phoenix (on Phoenix Road east from MD 45) and at Ashland (on Ashland Road east from MD 45).

Bicycle Repair Service

Monkton Bike Rental
1900 Monkton Road, Monkton
410-771-4058
Bikes, baby trailers, tubes, and canoes for rent

3

The Hills of Hampstead

Location: *Carroll County*
Terrain: *Hilly*
Road conditions: *Paved country roads with light traffic*
Distance: *13.2 miles*
Highlights: *The country towns of Hampstead and Snydersburg, Simmons Home Made Ice Cream Store, Cascade Lake*

Carroll County consists mainly of hilly farm country that hugs the Maryland–Pennsylvania line. Originally settled by people of English stock, the area soon saw an influx of German-speaking farmers from nearby Pennsylvania. Although the suburban sprawl of Greater Baltimore is making inroads, the county is still, by and large, rural. This tour loops through a corner of northeastern Carroll County, starting at North Carroll High School on MD 482 in Hampstead. After passing through the old-fashioned, front-porch town, it goes through farm country where cornfields and barns seem to be making a valiant stand against subdivisions. After a stop at an old-fashioned ice-cream store and a swim in a lake, the tour returns to Hampstead.

0.0   Leaving the parking lot of North Carroll High School, turn right on MD 482.

0.4   Turn right on Main Street (MD 30).

> Hampstead is a typical northern Maryland town, with rockers and geraniums on the front porches and flags flying even when it's not a holiday.

Cascade Lake, nestled in the hills of Hampstead,
invites cyclists to take a refreshing dip.

1.3 *Turn right on Houcksville Road.*

2.7 *Turn right on Hoffmans Mill Road, a pretty country byway that
runs through woods along a stream.*

5.3 *Turn right on Coon Club Road, which leads up a long hill and
into a suburban area.*

6.5 *Turn right on Gorsuch Road North, which leads down one long
hill and then, unfortunately, up another one.*

8.1 *Tall trees shade a rural graveyard to your left.*

30

8.7   At the intersection with MD 482, turn right. Then make an immediate left onto Cape Horn Road.

9.5   In the village of Snydersburg, turn right on Snydersburg Road, in front of St. Mark's Lutheran Church Parsonage.

9.7   Simmons store, to your right, has a little of everything, including hand-dipped ice-cream cones.

9.8   Cascade Lake, to your left, a spring-fed, six-acre natural lake, provides a good place for a refreshing swim in season.

Admission is charged, and there are changing rooms, a pleasant snack bar overlooking the lake, floats to swim to, and boats to rent.

10.5   Turn left on MD 482, then make an immediate right onto Brobeck Road.

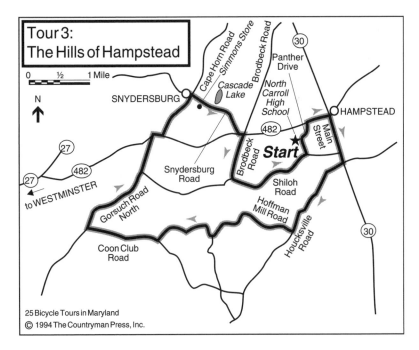

Tour 3:
The Hills of Hampstead

25 Bicycle Tours in Maryland
© 1994 The Countryman Press, Inc.

11.3   *Turn left on Shiloh Road, a hilly, partly wooded road.*

12.7   *To your left is Shiloh Antiques.*

12.8   *Turn left on Panther Drive (unmarked), which leads onto the high school grounds.*

13.2   *Return to North Carroll High School parking lot.*

Bicycle Repair Services

White's Bicycle
12 West Main Street, Westminster
410-848-3440
No rentals

4
The Streets of Baltimore

Location: *Baltimore City*
Terrain: *Mostly flat*
Road conditions: *City streets with light traffic on weekends*
Distance: *9.8 miles*
Highlights: *Fort McHenry, the Enoch Pratt Library, the Washington Monument, the Peale Museum, the Shot Tower, the Star-Spangled Banner House, Little Italy, the Inner Harbor*

The state song exhorts Marylanders to "avenge the patriotic gore/that flecks the streets of Baltimore," referring to an incident that took place just after the outbreak of the Civil War. On April 19, 1861, fifteen people were killed in a riot that broke out in this city of divided loyalties when a Massachusetts regiment was moved across town from one railroad station to another.

This tour leads bicyclists through those now peaceful streets, to attractions patriotic, literary, artistic, historic, religious, scientific, and gastronomic. It begins at the quintessential patriotic place—the fort that inspired a young lawyer named Francis Scott Key to write "The Star-Spangled Banner"—and makes its way to Mount Vernon Place, site of the Walters Art Gallery, the Peabody Conservatory of Music, and the first monument to honor George Washington. After a stop at the city history museum and visits to the Shot Tower and to the house where the flag that flew over Fort McHenry was sewn, the tour threads through Little Italy, where only the strong can resist a restaurant stop. Baltimore's popular Inner Harbor, with a heady variety of museum, shopping, and food attractions, is the last stop before returning to Fort McHenry.

Fort McHenry may be reached from I-95, through exit 55.

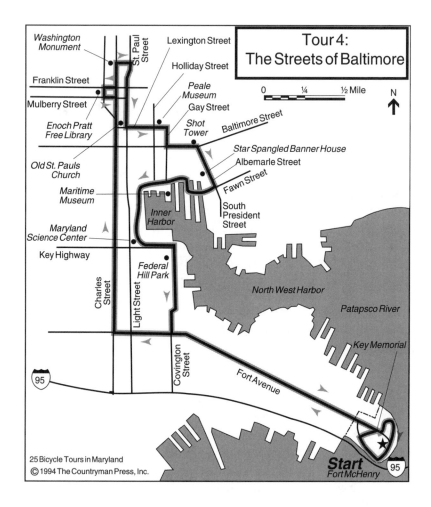

0.0 *From the parking lot next to the Visitor Center, turn right on the multipurpose trail along the Patapsco River.*

The truce ship from which Francis Scott Key saw the huge flag flying over Fort McHenry sat at anchor on the horizon, to your left.

0.2 *Lock your bike to a bench to visit the fort.*

Here valiant fighting in September 1814 sent the British fleet packing—first to Jamaica and then to New Orleans, where they finally lost the war.

There are frequent interpretative programs, and the Visitor Center provides an excellent film about the Battle of Baltimore.

0.6   *At the V, take the right path to a neoclassical statue honoring Francis Scott Key.*

Actually, the statue depicts Orpheus, the Greek god of music. When the statue was unveiled in 1922, President Warren G. Harding spoke, giving the first presidential speech broadcast on coast-to-coast radio. Continue to the park entry road and turn left.

1.0   *Exit the park and proceed straight ahead on Fort Avenue.*

This road crosses a railroad bridge, passes an interesting, vine-covered warehouse to your right, and travels through a traditional Baltimore blue-collar neighborhood with union halls and Permastone houses—some with marble stoops.

2.8   *Turn right on South Charles Street, which leads through the gentrified Federal Hill district, past several antique shops, into the downtown financial district.*

4.1   *To your right is Old St. Paul's.*

This basilica-style church was built in 1856 to serve a parish established in 1692. The architect, Richard Upjohn, also designed Trinity Church in New York City.

4.3   *Turn left on Franklin Street for one block.*

4.4   *Make another left on Cathedral Street.*

The neoclassical Enoch Pratt Free Library houses collected papers of two distinguished literary sons of Baltimore: H. L. Mencken and Edgar Allan Poe. Across the street stands the Basilica of the Assumption of the Blessed Virgin Mary, built between 1806 and 1821, the first Roman Catholic cathedral in the United States.

4.5   *Turn left on Mulberry Street.*

4.6   *Turn left on Charles Street.*

This street swoops down a hill and up another to the 164-foot Doric column topped by a 16-foot statue of George Washington.

To the left of the monument, across Charles Street, stands the Walters Art Gallery, with superb collections of classical, medieval, Renaissance, and Oriental art. To the right of the monument is the renowned Peabody Conservatory of Music, facing Mount Vernon Square, which could pass as the setting for a Masterpiece Theater series. Cross the square and turn right, in front of the Victorian gothic Mount Vernon Place Methodist Church, heading downhill on cobblestoned Mount Vernon Place.

4.9   *Turn right on St. Paul Street.*

Stop to admire the statue of Severn Teacke Wallis, a lawyer, poet, and ancestor of Wallis Warfield, the Baltimore girl who became the Duchess of Windsor.

5.4   *Turn left on Lexington Street.*

5.5   *Turn left on Holliday Street to the Municipal Museum of the City of Baltimore, also called the Peale Museum to your right.*

This museum, opened in 1814 by the artist brothers Rembrandt and Rubens Peale, was America's first museum. It featured paintings by the gallery owners and their father, Charles Wilson Peale, renowned portraitist of George Washington. It also included a "cabinet of natural history." Later the building served as City Hall and as the first public school for blacks. Zion Lutheran Church, adjacent to the museum and entered through a lovely

A monument to Francis Scott Key
adorns the grounds of Baltimore's Fort McHenry.

garden, is a red-brick, German gothic structure built in the 1840s. There is still a German-language Sunday service, and several German-born pastors are buried in the courtyard. Walk your bike through the courtyard to Gay Street.

5.6   *Turn right on Gay Street, walking your bike on the sidewalk.*

5.7   *Turn left on Baltimore Street.*

5.9   *Cross the Fallsway expressway at the light and continue to the Baltimore Shot Tower, on your left.*

The 215-foot red-brick tower was erected in 1828 for the purpose of manufacturing shot. The method was crude but effective: Molten lead poured through sieves from platforms near the top formed pellets that turned hard when they finally fell into a water "quenching" tank at the bottom. Continue on Baltimore Street just past the Shot Tower and take the first right, onto Albemarle Street.

6.1   *To your right, on the corner of Albemarle and Pratt streets, stands the Star-Spangled Banner House.*

Here, in 1813, Mary Young Pickersgill sewed the oversized flag that flew over Fort McHenry and inspired Key. Ms. Pickersgill was responding to a request from the fort's commandant, Major George Armistead, "to have a flag so large that the British will have no difficulty in seeing it from a distance." The banner, which measured 30 feet by 42 feet and took 400 yards of wool, now hangs in the Smithsonian Institution in Washington, DC. Continue down Albemarle Street into Little Italy, a treasure-trove of Italian restaurants. The house at 235 Albemarle, to your left, has a painted screen, a disappearing folk art. These hark back to the days before widespread air-conditioning. The scenery painted on the screen provided privacy while letting in fresh air.

6.2   *Turn right on Fawn Street.*

6.3   *Cross South President Street to Columbus Piazza, where a statue of the great explorer gazes out over Baltimore Harbor. Traverse the plaza and cross a bridge. Then ride around a circle and follow signs to a pedestrian bridge.*

> Before crossing the pedestrian bridge you may want to stop to look at the Seven Foot Knoll Lighthouse, which originally guarded the entrance to the harbor. Built in 1856, it is Maryland's oldest surviving screwpile lighthouse.

7.0   *After crossing two pedestrian bridges, you will be in the thick of Baltimore's Inner Harbor development.*

> You will have to guide your bike through the sea of pedestrians who flock here to visit the Aquarium, the Maritime Museum, the U.S.F. *Constellation*, or just to eat, shop, and ride the pedal boats.

7.3   *To your left, along the quai, a shuttle boat leaves for Fort McHenry every half-hour.*

> Sometimes, at the captain's discretion, it takes bicycles. If you want to return to the starting place by sea, inquire at the ticket kiosk.

7.4   *To your right is the Maryland Science Center, an excellent "hands on" museum.*

7.6   *Rash Park, to your right, contains a mast memorializing the captain and crew of the* **Pride of Baltimore,** *lost at sea in 1986. Walk through the park and carry your bike up the steps to the sidewalk along Key Highway and turn left.*

7.7   *Cross Key Highway at the light and turn right on Covington Street, which skirts Federal Hill Park.*

> From the top of the hill, the view of the city and harbor is spectacular. The hill is so named because a parade to

celebrate Maryland's ratification of the Constitution in 1788 ended here.

8.3   *Turn left on Fort Avenue.*

9.6   *Re-enter Fort McHenry.*

9.8   *Arrive back at the parking lot.*

Bicycle Repair Service

Light Street Cycles
1015 Light Street, Baltimore
410-685-2234
Rentals

GREATER
WASHINGTON

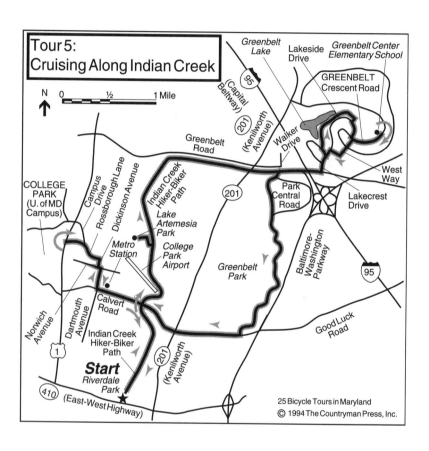

Tour 5:
Cruising Along Indian Creek

N
0   ½   1 Mile

Greenbelt Lake
Lakeside Drive
Greenbelt Center Elementary School
GREENBELT Crescent Road
(Capital Beltway)
95
Greenbelt Road
(201)
(Kenilworth Avenue)
Walker Drive
West Way
Park Central Road
Lakecrest Drive
COLLEGE PARK (U. of MD Campus)
Campus Drive
Rossborough Lane
Dickinson Avenue
Indian Creek Hiker-Biker Path
(201)
Lake Artemesia Park
Metro Station
College Park Airport
Greenbelt Park
Baltimore-Washington Parkway
95
Norwich Avenue
Dartmouth Avenue
Calvert Road
Indian Creek Hiker-Biker Path
(201)
(Kenilworth Avenue)
Good Luck Road
1
Start
Riverdale Park
410   (East-West Highway)

25 Bicycle Tours in Maryland
© 1994 The Countryman Press, Inc.

5
Indian Creek

Location: Prince George's County
Terrain: Flat to rolling
Road conditions: Paved trail, dirt trail, park road, some busy roads with varying shoulder room
Distance: 13.5 miles
Highlights: Indian Creek, College Park Airport, historic Greenbelt, Greenbelt Park, the University of Maryland

Indian Creek, part of the Northeast Branch of the Anacostia River, cuts a river of relative tranquillity through the suburban sprawl of Prince George's County. A hiker-biker path beside the stream is the jump-off point for this tour, which continues to Greenbelt, the art-deco darling of New Deal planners, cuts through wilderness-like Greenbelt Park, and visits the University of Maryland campus before returning to the starting point in Riverdale Park, off East-West Highway in Riverdale.

0.0 Leaving the parking lot, the trail leads under an overpass and along the creek, through wooded and marshy parkland.

0.7 At Calvert Road, the trail turns right, goes under a bridge, and continues on the other side.

0.9 College Park Airport, to your left, opened in 1911.

General "Hap" Arnold and other famous air corps officers were trained to be flying aces here. College Park Airport was also the terminus of the first airmail flights between New York, Philadelphia, and Washington. Still a busy field, it now serves mainly small planes.

1.1 *Lake Artemesia Park, to your left, was created by Metro in order to obtain fill to raise the track bed on a nearby section of Metrorail.*

After digging the fill material from this site, Metro engineers created two lakes—one for recreation and one as a wildlife habitat. There are rest rooms, an observation platform, trails, and a basin for radio-controlled boats. A bonus is that Metro saved an estimated $3 million by digging here rather than by hauling fill from elsewhere.

After visiting the park, continue on the trail by crossing the creek on the bridge to your right. Once across the bridge, turn left.

3.0 *The trail emerges from the woods at Greenbelt Road, which has so many fast-food outlets you can actually smell them while still on the trail. Turn right on Greenbelt Road, which is busy but has a sidewalk.*

3.8 *When the sidewalk ends, either ride on the grass or cross the road and use the sidewalk on the other side.*

4.6 *Turn left on Lakecrest Drive and follow a marked bike route into the community of Greenbelt.*

4.9 *When the road ends at Greenbelt Lake, turn right along a dirt and gravel trail along the lake.*

5.6 *Leave the trail at the east entrance to the park and turn right on Lakeside Drive, which climbs a slight hill.*

5.8 *At the top of the hill turn left on Crescent Road South.*

5.9 *Greenbelt Center Elementary School, to your left, is an excellent example of the "moderne," streamlined architecture favored by New Deal planners.*

Walk your bike up to the school to get a closer look at the bas-reliefs, by Works Progress Administration (WPA) sculptor Lenore Thomas. The unifying theme of the reliefs is the Preamble to the Constitution, and Thomas used

INSURE DOMESTIC TRANQUILLITY

The Preamble to the Constitution inspired the bas-relief sculpture on this school in the planned New Deal town of Greenbelt.

working-class people, rather than Greek gods, to illustrate it.

6.0 Greenbelt Center is to your left.

The center was designed to look like the Main Street of an American small town but to offer additional amenities—a pedestrian mall, park-like seating areas, and shopping and entertainment facilities in a cluster. Although less flamboyant than the school, the movie theater and shops are also in the Art Moderne style. Centerpiece of the complex is a statue, "Mother and Child," by Lenore Thomas.

The model town of Greenbelt, planned and built by the Resettlement Administration of the Department of Agriculture, was one of three such social experiments actually completed. (The others are Greendale, Wisconsin, and Greenhills, Ohio). The idea was that people migrating from country to city should have green satellite towns to live in—places that combined the best of rural and urban life. Between 1935 and 1938, houses and apartments for about 3,000 people were constructed here, in "moderne" motifs featuring glass brick and aluminum casement windows. Originally rented from the government, the homes are now privately owned. After a stop at Greenbelt Center, turn right on Crescent Road South.

6.3 *The Greenbelt Museum, to your left, houses artifacts of the community's history.*

6.4 *Turn left on Westway.*

6.7 *Turn right on Lakeside Drive.*

6.8 *Turn left on Lakecrest Drive.*

7.0 *Turn right on Greenbelt Road.*

7.4 *At Walker Drive, cross Greenbelt road at the light and enter Greenbelt Park.*

This thousand-acre woodland, run by the National Park Service, offers camping, picnicking, and hiking.

7.5 *Just past the park headquarters, turn right on Park Central Road, which leads up and down hills through woods thick with dogwood.*

8.9 *The road ends, but a paved bicycle trail continues.*

9.4 *The trail ends on Good Luck Road. Turn right on this often busy road.*

10.1 *After crossing Kenilworth Avenue (MD 201), Good Luck Road becomes Calvert Road.*

11.0 *At the College Park Metro Station, walk your bike through the tunnel and then cross the railroad tracks at the signal.*

11.1 *Turn right on Dartmouth Avenue.*

11.3 *Turn left on Norwich Avenue.*

11.4 At the intersection with Dickinson Avenue, turn right into the dormitory parking lot. At the end of the lot, bear left on the sidewalk past the garden apartment–style dorms.

11.5 Turn left on Rossborough Lane.

11.7 Cross US 1 and enter the University of Maryland main campus.

> The 500-acre campus was built in the Georgian style, with many later additions. The Rossborough Inn, a brick tavern built along this old post road in 1799, now serves as a faculty club. Just to the north, the Dairy Science Salesroom (open weekdays only) sells ice cream made by students in the agricultural school. After visiting the campus, retrace your route, crossing US 1 onto Rossborough Lane.

12.0 Turn right on Dickinson Avenue.

12.1 Turn left on Norwich Avenue.

12.2 Turn right on Dartmouth Avenue.

12.4 Turn left on Calvert Road and follow it across the railroad tracks. After walking your bike through the Metro tunnel, continue on Calvert Road.

12.7 Turn right into the park and onto the Indian Creek trail.

13.5 Return to Riverdale Park.

Bicycle Repair Services

Riverdale Cycle and Fitness
4503 Queensbury Road, Riverdale
301-864-4731
No rentals

Proteus Bike and Fitness
9217 Baltimore Boulevard, College Park
301-441-2929
Rentals

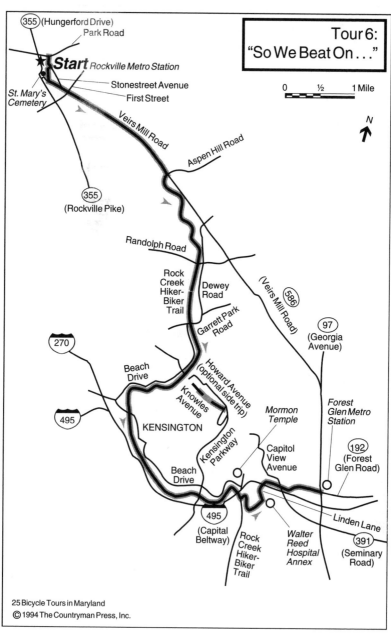

355 (Hungerford Drive)
Park Road

★ **Start** Rockville Metro Station

Stonestreet Avenue
First Street

St. Mary's Cemetery

Veirs Mill Road

Aspen Hill Road

355 (Rockville Pike)

Randolph Road

Rock Creek Hiker-Biker Trail

Dewey Road

Garrett Park Road

(Veirs Mill Road)

586

97 (Georgia Avenue)

270

Beach Drive

Howard Avenue (optional side trip)

Knowles Avenue

KENSINGTON

495

Beach Drive

Kensington Parkway

Mormon Temple

Capitol View Avenue

Forest Glen Metro Station

192 (Forest Glen Road)

495 (Capital Beltway)

Rock Creek Hiker-Biker Trail

Walter Reed Hospital Annex

Linden Lane

391 (Seminary Road)

**Tour 6:
"So We Beat On . . ."**

0   ½   1 Mile

N ↑

25 Bicycle Tours in Maryland
© 1994 The Countryman Press, Inc.

48

6

"So We Beat On…"

Location: Montgomery County
Terrain: Flat to rolling
Road conditions: Paved roads with shoulders on busy roads and a
paved trail
Distance: 13.2 miles
Highlights: The graves of Scott and Zelda Fitzgerald, the Rock Creek
Hiker-Biker Trail, the romantic architecture of Forest Glen

This tour begins at the Rockville Metro Station, a few pedals away from
St. Mary's Cemetery, final resting place of Jazz Age legends Scott and
Zelda Fitzgerald. The inscription on Francis Scott Key Fitzgerald's tomb-
stone is the last line of his blockbuster novel *The Great Gatsby*: "So we
beat on, boats against the current, borne back ceaselessly into the past."

After visiting the graves, the tour beats on, down a short stretch of
busy Veirs Mill Road, and then enters the verdant Rock Creek Hiker-
Biker Trail, which follows its namesake creek and emerges from the
woods at intervals in meadows used as soccer and baseball fields. After
a dramatic vista of the Mormon Temple, the tour follows a side trail to
Forest Glen Annex of Walter Reed Hospital, a goldmine of eccentric
buildings left over from a turn-of-the-century finishing school. The
tour ends at Forest Glen Metro Station, whence the Metro will bear you
effortlessly back to the starting point.

If you don't have a Metro bicycle pass (see Introduction, "About
Metrorail"), you can still do this tour by parking in the Rockville Metro
lot (free on weekends) and, at the end of the tour, locking your bike at
Forest Glen while you return to Rockville on the Metro to get your car.

0.0 Exit the Rockville Metro Station onto South Stonestreet Avenue and turn right.

0.2 To your right you will see a short flight of steps leading to a pedestrian bridge over the Metro tracks. Carry your bike up the steps and across the bridge. At the end of the bridge, turn right, riding on the sidewalk to the St. Mary's Church complex, to your right. Take the driveway past both the modern church and the old church (built in 1817) to the cemetery.

The numerous Fitzgerald graves are found near the back of the cemetery, surrounded by boxwood and shaded by old oaks.

Although F. Scott Fitzgerald was born in St. Paul, Minnesota, his family had deep roots in Maryland and was related to "Star-Spangled Banner" author Francis Scott Key. When he died in 1940 the poet laureate of the Roaring Twenties was not in good standing with the Roman Catholic Church, which refused to allow him to be buried among his ancestors at St. Mary's. Instead, he was exiled to a nonsectarian burying ground a few miles away. Years later, after the church had mellowed a bit, both Scott and Zelda, who died in a 1948 fire at a mental hospital, were moved to the Fitzgerald plot at St. Mary's. Their daughter, Scotty, joined them in 1986.

Although the cemetery stands at a very busy, three-road intersection, the tall trees and the adjacent old brick church lend a certain tranquillity. One is reminded of a passage in Fitzgerald's *Tender is the Night*, in which Dick Diver attends his father's funeral:

...at the churchyard his father was laid among a hundred Divers, Dorseys, and Hunters. It was very friendly leaving him there with all his relations around him. Flowers were scattered on the brown unsettled earth. Dick had no more ties there now and did not believe he would come back...

Jazz Age figures Scott and Zelda Fitzgerald rest in the churchyard at St. Mary's in Rockville.

Fitzgerald, however, did come back, albeit by a circuitous route.

0.4 *After visiting the cemetery, exit the church grounds and turn left, retracing your path past the footbridge and riding on the sidewalk along busy Veirs Mill Road (MD 586), which goes over the Metro tracks on a bridge. At the first traffic light, cross Veirs Mill Road and continue on the sidewalk on the other side.*

When the sidewalk ends, there is a frontage road, and when that ends, there is a shoulder.

3.2 *At the intersection with Aspen Hill Road, turn right onto the Rock Creek Hiker-Biker Trail, which winds through a narrow greenbelt all the way to Washington.*

The trail is paved and well marked. At intervals the woods give way to groomed meadows where you can stop to watch a soccer game in practice—often a skilled and spirited contest between members of one of the area's immigrant communities.

7.0 *At the intersection with Knowles Avenue, you can turn left and go 0.7 mile to the Howard Avenue antique district of Kensington.*

This will add 1.4 miles to your trip.

11.0 *Almost directly in front of you looms the Mormon Temple, an exuberant, soaring white marble structure topped by a bronze trumpeting angel, Moroni.*

Mormons believe that Moroni lived in America in the fourth century A.D. and compiled the Book of Mormon. It was Moroni who appeared to Joseph Smith in 1827 and instructed him to found the Church of Jesus Christ of Latter-day Saints. The temple, completed in 1974, has an Oz-like quality which once prompted a prankster to scrawl "Surrender Dorothy" on its fence.

11.5 *At the sign for the Walter Reed Annex and Forest Glen Metro, turn left, following the "bike route" signs and keeping left.*

This will take you onto the grounds of the Walter Reed Army Hospital's Forest Glen Annex.

12.1 *After leaving the bike trail, turn left on Linden Lane.*

Originally a resort, Forest Glen was acquired in 1894 for use as a girls' finishing school, the National Park Seminary. Over the next thirty years or so, a series of eccentric buildings were constructed to house the students.

12.3 *At the intersection with Woodstock Avenue, continue on Linden Lane.*

12.4 *The shingled Japanese pagoda on your right, now a private residence, was once a sorority house. Follow Linden Lane down the hill, out of the annex grounds, and across the Beltway.*

12.6 *Turn right on Forest Glen Road.*

12.9 *Turn left into the Forest Glen Metro Station.*

Bicycle Repair Services

The Bicycle Place
13605 Connecticut Avenue, Aspen Hill
301-460-0420
No rentals

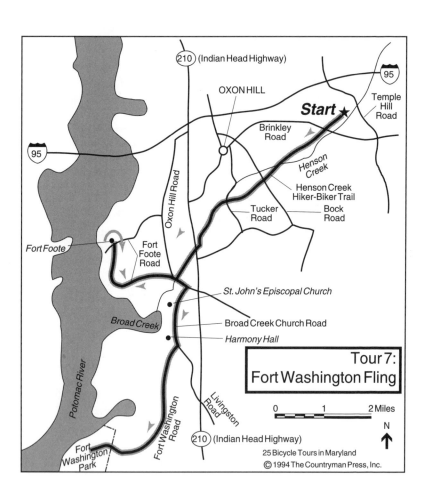

210 (Indian Head Highway)

95

OXON HILL

Start ★

Temple Hill Road

Brinkley Road

Henson Creek

Henson Creek Hiker-Biker Trail

95

Oxon Hill Road

Tucker Road

Bock Road

Fort Foote

Fort Foote Road

St. John's Episcopal Church

Broad Creek

Broad Creek Church Road

Harmony Hall

Potomac River

Livingston Road

Fort Washington Road

Fort Washington Park

210 (Indian Head Highway)

Tour 7:
Fort Washington Fling

0   1   2 Miles

N

25 Bicycle Tours in Maryland
© 1994 The Countryman Press, Inc.

7
Fort Washington Fling

Location: Prince George's County
Terrain: Moderately hilly
Road conditions: Off-road bike trail, suburban streets, park roads
Distance: 16.6 miles
Highlights: The Henson Creek Trail, Fort Foote, St. John's Church,
Fort Washington

The Henson Creek Hiker-Biker Trail runs downstream from Oxon Hill through wooded parkland. The creek flows into Broad Creek and then into the Potomac River, but the trail stops short. The tour follows suburban streets to the remains of Fort Foote, a battlement built to defend the city of Washington during the Civil War. Next stop is the historic St. John's Episcopal Church at Broad Creek, where Washington worshiped. The tour ends at Fort Washington, designed by the cantankerous Pierre L'Enfant, who laid out the federal city.

0.0 *Pick up the trail at the end of Old Temple Hills Road, off Temple Hill Road just north of Brinkley Road.*

> The trail travels through woods and meadows, following the stream.

0.8 *Emerging from parkland, the trail continues on the other side of Brinkley Road, a little to the right.*

2.8 *The trail crosses Bock Road and continues through park land, leading around a small lake.*

> There are rest rooms near the tennis courts.

4.0   *At the Tucker Road Ice Rink, cross Tucker Road and pick up the trail again, a little to the left.*

This is the prettiest part of the trail, through woods and marshland and across the stream on arched wooden bridges.

6.0   *The trail passes under Indian Head Highway, reemerges behind some suburban backyards, and leads up a small hill.*

7.0   *The trail ends at Oxon Hill Road. Turn right on Oxon Hill Road and then make an immediate left onto South Fort Foote Road, which winds through a suburban neighborhood.*

8.3   *Look left for views of the Potomac River.*

8.8   *Turn left into Fort Foote Park and follow a dirt path to the ruins of Fort Foote.*

Named for Rear Admiral Andrew Hull Foote, who died of wounds suffered in the Mississippi River campaign, this was one of the most elaborate and best-equipped of the 68 forts built to protect the capital from the Confederates. The earthworks garrison, high on a bluff above the Potomac, was visited by many dignitaries, including Lincoln himself. On one occasion, Lincoln and his party traveled down the river on a paddlewheeler and were entertained at the fort by its commandant, who was Secretary Seward's son. The dignitaries ate local peaches, washed down with champagne. The fort's heavy guns, which weighed 49,000 pounds, could fire 500-pound cannon balls three miles down the river. The fort's prowess was never tested, for no hostile forces sailed up the Potomac. Its only casualties were due to malaria. The fort was abandoned in 1878 and left to ruin. During the 1980s, it was partially restored, with some of the 15-inch Rodman guns remounted.

Built in 1824 on the Potomac River to guard the nation's capital, Fort Washington is now a national park.

9.1 *After visiting the fort, exit the park and backtrack on Fort Foote Road.*

10.8 *Turn right on Oxon Hill Road, watching for traffic as you descend a hill.*

11.2 *Turn right on Broad Creek Church Road to St. John's Episcopal Church, which dates from 1766.*

"Credible evidence and honest tradition record that Washington attended services here on numerous occasions," reads the historical marker. Mount Vernon lies a short cruise across the Potomac, and a trip to St. John's would have been easier than an overland coach trip. In the churchyard are graves of three Revolutionary War soldiers.

11.5 Exit the church grounds on Old St. John's Way.

11.6 Turn right on Livingston Road. Watch for traffic.

12.4 On your right is Harmony Hall, currently under restoration.

The two-and-a-half-story Georgian brick house, built about 1750, was originally named Battersea. The name was changed after the locally prominent Addison brothers brought their brides here in 1792. The two couples lived here in such harmony that the house was rechristened.

12.9 Turn right on Fort Washington Road.

15.8 At the top of the hill, look right for a view of the river with the Washington Monument in the distance.

16.4 Enter Fort Washington Park, a National Park Service property.

16.6 Arrive at the Visitor Center and the fort.

Built in 1808 as Fort Warburton, the fort was built to protect the capital from the British if tensions between the two nations grew into a full-fledged war, which they did. On August 20, 1814, British warships sailed up the Potomac. Fort Warburton's commandant, Captain Samuel Dyson, evacuated his men and blew up the fort so it wouldn't fall into British hands. Reconstruction began almost immediately, under the direction of the temperamental Pierre L'Enfant, the architect who planned the capital city. L'Enfant's inability to get along with the powers that held the purse strings—plus diminishing interest in defense after the Treaty of Ghent—strung out the project, which was finally completed, though not yet armed, in 1824. Twenty-some years later, with sectional tensions rising, the fortifications were strengthened and cannons were installed to defend the capital against a waterborne Confederate attack, which never occurred. Today, visitors can walk across the drawbridge and under the magnificent stone arch into the parade grounds, lined by barracks and officers' quarters. From the ramparts, there are wonderful views in all directions. The park also has a lighthouse, picnic areas, miles of trails and sports facilities.

Bicycle Repair Service

Clinton Bicycle
8935 Woodyard Road, Clinton
301-868-0033
No rentals

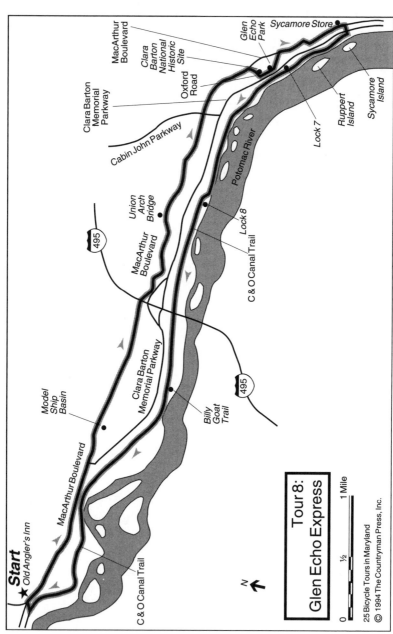

Start
★ Old Angler's Inn

MacArthur Boulevard

C & O Canal Trail

Model Ship Basin

495

MacArthur Boulevard

Union Arch Bridge

Clara Barton Memorial Parkway

Billy Goat Trail

495

Lock 8

C & O Canal Trail

Cabin John Parkway

Clara Barton Memorial Parkway

MacArthur Boulevard

Clara Barton National Historic Site

Oxford Road

Glen Echo Park

Sycamore Store

Potomac River

Lock 7

Ruppert Island

Sycamore Island

N ←

0   ½   1 Mile

**Tour 8:
Glen Echo Express**

25 Bicycle Tours in Maryland
© 1994 The Countryman Press, Inc.

8
Glen Echo Express

Location: *Montgomery County*
Terrain: *Flat*
Road conditions: *Paved, side-of-the-road bike path, and unpaved canal towpath*
Distance: *12.6 miles*
Highlights: *The Clara Barton House, Glen Echo Park, the Chesapeake & Ohio Canal, the Old Angler's Inn*

For the first sixty-some years of the twentieth century, people used to take the street car from downtown Washington to Glen Echo, to ride the carousel, swim in the Crystal Pool, dance in the Spanish Ballroom. Even earlier, the park served as a chautauqua. The streetcars are gone, but the park remains as an arts center, and the carousel has been preserved.

This tour begins in the parking lot of the Old Angler's Inn—on MacArthur Boulevard north of I-495—and follows a dedicated, on-road bicycle path to the park, stopping at the former home of American Red Cross founder Clara Barton. After a refreshment break at the old-time Sycamore Store, the tour makes its way to the Chesapeake & Ohio Canal towpath and loops back to the starting point. Recent criminal activity on the towpath underlines the need for caution. See the section on "Safety" in the Introduction to this book.

0.0 *Leave the parking lot and turn right, heading south on the marked bicycle path along MacArthur Boulevard.*

This artery used to be called Conduit Road, for the pipes

under it that carried water from Great Falls to the now vanished Georgetown Reservoir. The system was designed by soldier-engineer Montgomery Cunningham Meigs, who took his task very seriously. When given the assignment in 1852 by then Secretary of War Jefferson Davis, he said: "Let us show that the rulers chosen by the people are not less careful of the safety, health, and beauty of their capital than the emperors who caused their names to be remembered with respect and affection by those who still drink the water supplied by their magnificent aqueducts."

1.1 *Stop and walk your bike across the entrance road to the Clara Barton Parkway.*

1.4 *The long, hangar-like buildings on your right house a model ship basin, in which scale models of Navy ships are tested.*

2.6 *MacArthur Boulevard passes under the Capital Beltway (I-495).*

3.1 *The bike path crosses MacArthur Boulevard, runs through woods and crosses the Union Arch bridge.*

The bridge was constructed between 1857 and 1864 over Cabin John Creek, a tributary of the Potomac. At the time of construction, this was, at 220 feet, the longest single-arch span in the world. It is made of local sandstone and Massachusetts granite.

3.5 *The small shopping center to your left includes a bicycle shop and a food shop.*

4.6 *Look to the right for the remains of an old railroad trestle, visible through the woods.*

There are off-again, on-again plans to turn this right of way into a hiker-biker trail.

5.0 *Turn right on Oxford Road to the Clara Barton National Historical Site, run by the National Park Service.*

Built in 1891 partially of boards salvaged from the

Johnstown Flood, the yellow frame house first served as a
Red Cross warehouse and then as both home and office
for American Red Cross founder Clara Barton. A clerk in
the US Patent Office, Barton volunteered to nurse Civil
War wounded when the office was turned into a field
hospital. After the war, she helped locate missing soldiers
and lobbied the government to adopt the Geneva
Convention. In 1881 she became president of the
American Red Cross and worked tirelessly on every
disaster that came along. In 1904, after a bitter
disagreement with President Theodore Roosevelt over the
American Red Cross performance during the Spanish–
American War, Barton retired to Glen Echo, where she
kept a horse, cows, and chickens. She died in the house
in 1912. After visiting the Barton house, continue across
the parking lot to Glen Echo Park.

**5.3   *Cross Minnehaha Creek on a wooden bridge and follow the
path into Glen Echo Park.***

The first organized activity on this site began in 1891,
when the Baltzley brothers established the Chautauqua
Assembly "to promote liberal and practical education,
especially among the masses of the people," and, not
incidentally, to sell lots and houses to the same masses.
Promoted as the "Rhineland of the Potomac," the
Assembly dissolved after rumors that one of the teachers
there had died of malaria. After a few moribund years, the
site blossomed as an amusement park, with rides, a
ballroom, and a pool that held 3,000 people. After a
popular, 60-year run, the park closed in 1968. The
National Park Service took over in 1971. It rents space to
various arts groups and still runs the historic Dentzel
Carousel, brought to the park in 1921.

**5.6   *Passing to the left of the stone tower, the only building
remaining from the Chautauqua period, carry your bike up a***

The tree-shaded Chesapeake & Ohio Canal towpath, once trod by barge-pulling mules, now draws cyclists, joggers, and hikers.

short flight of steps to the MacArthur Boulevard bicycle path and turn right.

5.7 *The charming Inn at Glen Echo, to your right, was formerly a roadhouse called Trav's where generations of local teens carved their initials in the wooden booths.*

6.4 *The Sycamore Store, across MacArthur Boulevard, makes sandwiches and sells sodas. From the store, re-cross MacArthur Boulevard and follow a well-worn path through the woods to a winding concrete bridge that carries you across the Clara Barton Parkway to a wooden bridge across the canal.*

6.6 *After carrying your bike up some steps, across the bridge, and down the steps on the towpath side of the canal, go north on the towpath for the return trip.*

6.7 *To your left, in the Potomac, lies Sycamore Island.*

The three-and-a-half-acre island has been owned by the Montgomery Sycamore Island Club since 1885. Members pull themselves to the island on a raft attached to a rope. Just north of Sycamore Island are Ruppert Island and several smaller nameless isles. Naturalists treasure these islands for their profusion of such aquatic plants as water willow and rose mallow, a wild hibiscus. Red-winged blackbirds and warblers nest on the islands, and ducks hang out here, too, probably to get the leavings of club parties on Sycamore Island.

7.2 *To your right is Lock 7, with a bridge leading to the lock keeper's house.*

8.6 *Lock 8 is the first of a series known as "Seven Locks."*

The locks collectively raise the canal 56 feet in a linear distance of a mile and a quarter. The lock keeper for Lock 8 earned an extra $50 a year to tend Locks 9 and 10.

9.6 *The towpath passes under the Capital Beltway, which goes directly over Lock 13.*

10.2 *To your left is the downriver entrance to the Billy Goat Trail, a popular hiking path.*

12.6 *Turn right on a causeway leading across the canal to the parking lot by the Old Angler's Inn.*

> The Old Angler's Inn, an excellent and fashionable restaurant, once turned away a group of hikers including Supreme Court Justice William O. Douglas because of dress code violations. Now, hikers and bikers are welcome to eat on the terrace.

Bicycle Repair Service

Proteus Bike and Fitness
7945 MacArthur Boulevard, Cabin John
301-229-5900
Rentals

ANNAPOLIS
AREA

9
Capital-to-Capital Express

Location: *Prince George's and Anne Arundel Counties*
Terrain: *Moderately hilly*
Road conditions: *Paved roads, a few with heavy traffic*
Distance: *64.5 miles*
Highlights: *Historic Annapolis, the U.S. Naval Academy, Maryland's Capitol, St. John's College, London Town Publik House and Gardens*

Annapolis has been a capital for a much longer time than has Washington—since 1694. And it is one of several cities that served as temporary capital of the new United States. The Continental Congress ratified the Treaty of Paris here, officially ending the Revolution. Since then, Annapolis has been invaded by armies of legislators, Naval Academy Middies and their more counterculture counterparts at St. John's College, boaters, and yachting wannabes, but it has retained the flavor of a colonial port city and kept most of its original architecture intact.

In fair weather, the highway to Annapolis from Washington is paved with blocked traffic. Fortunately, you can get there by bicycle—on much more pleasant roads.

The tour begins at the New Carrollton Metro station, which you can get to by Metro (see the Introduction, "About Metrorail") or where you can park your car free on weekends.

0.0   Exit the New Carrollton Metro station on the east side, following the bus lane. Turn right onto Garden City Drive, then left at the V, under US 50. Continue to the left on Ardwick Ardmore Road.

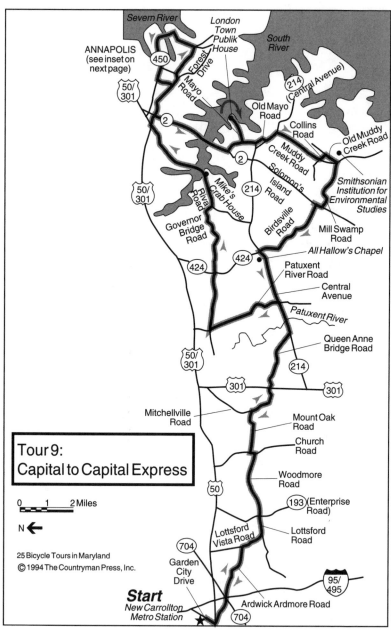

Tour 9:
Capital to Capital Express

0   1   2 Miles

N ←

25 Bicycle Tours in Maryland
© 1994 The Countryman Press, Inc.

Start
New Carrollton
Metro Station

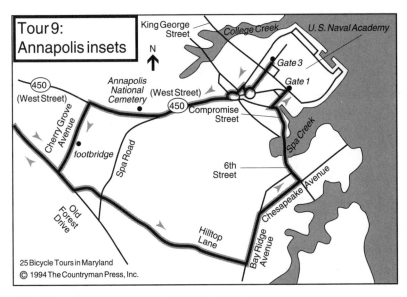

**Tour 9:
Annapolis insets**

N

King George
Street

College Creek

U. S. Naval Academy

Gate 3

Gate 1

*Annapolis
National
Cemetery*

(West Street)

450
(West Street)

450

Compromise
Street

Spa Creek

Cherry Grove
Avenue

footbridge

Spa Road

6th
Street

Chesapeake
Avenue

Old
Forest
Drive

Hilltop
Lane

Bay Ridge
Avenue

25 Bicycle Tours in Maryland

© 1994 The Countryman Press, Inc.

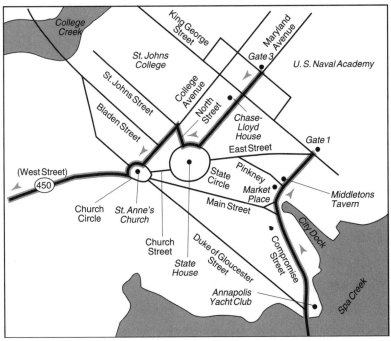

*College
Creek*

King George
Street

Maryland
Avenue

*St. Johns
College*

Gate 3

U. S. Naval Academy

St. Johns Street

College
Avenue

North
Street

Bladen Street

*Chase-
Lloyd
House*

Gate 1

East Street

(West Street)

450

Pinkney

State
Circle

Market
Place

*Middletons
Tavern*

Church
Circle

*St. Anne's
Church*

Main Street

Compromise
Street

City Dock

Church
Street

Duke of Gloucester
Street

*State
House*

*Annapolis
Yacht Club*

Spa Creek

3.4 Ardwick Ardmore Road ends in front of the Enterprise Golf Club. Turn right on Lottsford Vista Road. This will take you down a hill and along a pleasant stream.

4.2 Lottsford Vista Road ends. Turn left on Lottsford Road, which climbs a mild hill.

4.8 Lottsford Road ends at Enterprise Road (MD 193). Cross Enterprise Road at the light and continue straight on Woodmore Road.

5.3 The white clapboard Holy Family Church, set amidst tall trees, dates from 1890.

7.3 At Mount Oak Cemetery, turn left on Church Road.

7.4 At Mount Oak Methodist Church, built in 1881, turn right on Mount Oak Road, a rolling, country road.

8.9 Turn right on Mitchellville Road, after stopping at the convenience store at the intersection for refreshment.

This is a busy road, but there are little-used sidewalks.

10.3 Cross both lanes of US 301—very carefully. On the other side of the highway, Mitchellville Road turns into Queen Anne Bridge Road, which winds up a hill and through a rural area.

12.5 Turn left on Central Avenue (MD 214). Watch for traffic as you follow this busy road across the Patuxent River on a bridge.

13.7 Turn left on Patuxent River Road, which follows the river.

The road, and the river, are lined with sand and gravel operations, which contribute to the problems of the Chesapeake Bay. On weekends, however, the road is quiet and pleasant.

17.0 Turn right on Governor Bridge Road.

21.8 Turn left on Riva Road.

Since Annapolis is located on a neck, accessible only by a

A statue of Chief Tecumseh, copied from the figurehead of the USS *Delaware*, presides over the U.S. Naval Academy campus.

few roads, there are no low-traffic roads to get there from here. Use caution.

23.3 *After Mike's Crab House, to your right, watch for storm grates on the bridge.*

Mike's is a good place to refresh yourself and sample local specialties. It sits on the banks of the South River and affords great views from the deck and dock.

26.0 *Turn right on Forest Drive.*

27.8 *Bear left on Hilltop Lane and follow it through a residential area.*

29.1 *Turn left on Bay Ridge Avenue.*

29.5 *At the V, bear right on Chesapeake Avenue.*

29.8 *Turn left on Sixth Street, which leads to a bridge across Spa Creek and becomes Compromise Street.*

You may not be able to see the waters of Spa Creek because of the proverbial forest of masts. On your right, as soon as you cross the bridge, is the Annapolis Yacht Club.

30.1 *Just past the Annapolis Summer Garden Theater, to your left, at a small circle, turn right on Randall Street.*

On your right is the City Dock, where fisherfolk have been almost totally supplanted by the Top Sider set. On your left is a 1970 replacement of the Market House that had stood in this space since 1728. The current building holds food stands. Just beyond the Market House is the Middleton Tavern, whose all-header bond facade testifies to its early eighteenth-century origin. It once served as a custom house and is now serving its original function as a watering place and restaurant.

30.3 *Turn left in front of the Middleton, then make a sharp left onto Pinckney Street.*

At 18 Pinckney Street stands the Slicer-Shiplap House, which dates from 1723 and was built with ship planking. Retrace your way to Randall Street, which leads to the US Naval Academy gate.

30.5 Enter the Academy grounds (bike helmets required).

At a visitors center to your right you may sign up for a guided tour, or you may ride around on your own. Of special note is the domed chapel, whose stained-glass windows honor naval heroes, and a crypt containing the sarcophagus of John Paul Jones. The father of the American Navy died in Paris in 1792, after a stint in Russia where he was reportedly the lover of Catherine the Great. His remains were moved to Annapolis in 1905.

31.5 Exit the Academy through Gate 3 onto Maryland Avenue, a narrow cobblestoned street.

On your right, after crossing King George Street, you will see the Chase-Lloyd House, a Georgian mansion from Annapolis's "golden age," the late eighteenth century.

31.7 Climbing a slight hill, Maryland Avenue runs into State Circle.

State Circle is the site of the State House, completed just after the Revolution. It is open for tours daily.

31.9 At about 2 o'clock on State Circle, turn right on North Street and follow it one block.

32.0 Cross College Avenue and enter the campus of St. John's College.

St. John's dates from colonial times and bases its curriculum on the reading of great books. The Liberty Tree, on the lawn facing College Avenue, is a venerable tulip poplar that shaded revolutionary conspirators against the British. After leaving the campus, turn left on College Avenue and follow it to Church Circle, named for St. Anne's Church to your right, completed in 1792.

A cobblestone street leads to Maryland's State House.

32.2 At 12 o'clock on the circle, turn right on West Street (MD 450). Watch for traffic.

33.0 On your right is Annapolis National Cemetery, final resting place of many unknown Civil War soldiers.

33.5 Turn left on Cherry Grove Avenue, which is not a through street for cars. Cyclists may take advantage of a footbridge, however.

34.1 Turn right on Forest Drive.

35.4 Turn left on Solomons Island Road (MD 2). Ride on the shoulder.

38.2 Cross the South River on a bridge.

39.3 Turn left on Mayo Road.

40.1 Turn left on London Town Road.

41.3 At the end of the road, turn left into the London Town Publik House and Gardens.

> The attraction is open except January and February and Mondays. There is an admission fee.
>
> An early eighteenth-century boom town, London Town was the site of a ferry across the South River to Annapolis. The Publik House was built c. 1760 by ferry operator William Brown to house and feed waiting passengers. Docents give excellent tours, and the surrounding gardens are spectacular. After touring the house and gardens, double back on London Town Road.

43.1 Turn left on Mayo Road.

43.5 Bear left on Old Mayo Road.

43.9 Turn left on Central Avenue (MD 214).

44.3 Turn right on Muddy Creek Road.

46.2 Turn left on Collins Road.

46.5 Turn right on Old Muddy Creek Road, which skirts the Smithsonian Institution for Environmental Studies.

This facility gives programs for school and other groups.

46.6 Old Muddy Creek Road crosses Muddy Creek Road and becomes Mill Swamp Road, which climbs a hill.

48.4 Turn right on Solomons Island Road (MD 2). Watch for traffic.

48.6 Turn left on Birdsville Road.

51.6 Turn left on Central Avenue (MD 214). A market and deli are at the intersection.

51.8 All Hallows Chapel, on your right, has an inviting graveyard in which to eat the food purchased at the market.

54.3 Cross the Patuxent River on a bridge.

54.8 Turn right on Queen Anne Bridge Road.

56.0 After crossing US 301, Queen Anne Bridge Road becomes Mitchellville Road.

57.4 Turn left on Mount Oak Road.

58.9 Turn left on Church Road.

59.0 Turn right on Woodmore Road.

59.4 Cross Enterprise Road and continue straight on Lottsford Road.

60.0 Turn right on Lottsford Vista Road.

60.9 Turn left on Ardwick-Ardmore Road.

63.9 Turn right on Pennsy Drive and go over a bridge.

64.2 Turn left on Corporate Drive.

64.5 Enter Metro station.

Bicycle Repair Services

Capitol Bicycle Center
25 Old Solomons Island Road, Annapolis
410-266-5510
No rentals

Accommodations

Historic Inns of Annapolis
800-638-8902 in Maryland, 800-847-8882 out of Maryland

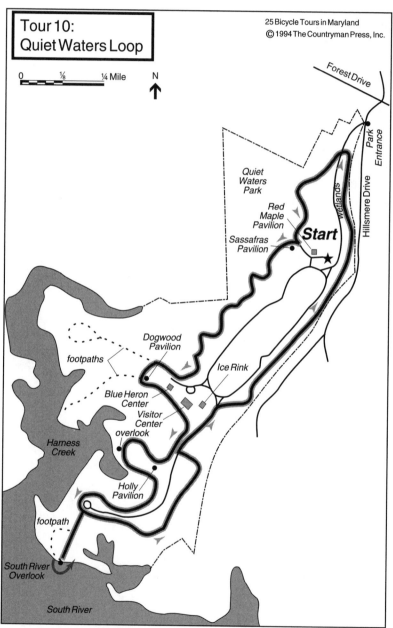

**Tour 10:
Quiet Waters Loop**

25 Bicycle Tours in Maryland
© 1994 The Countryman Press, Inc.

0   ⅛   ¼ Mile

N

Forest Drive

Quiet
Waters
Park

Red
Maple
Pavilion

Sassafras
Pavilion

Start

Wetlands

Park
Entrance

Hillsmere Drive

Dogwood
Pavilion

footpaths

Ice Rink

Blue Heron
Center

Visitor
Center
overlook

Harness
Creek

Holly
Pavilion

footpath

South River
Overlook

South River

10
Quiet Waters Loop

Location: Anne Arundel County
Terrain: Flat to rolling
Road conditions: Paved bike path and park road
Distance: 5.2 miles
Highlights: The Visitor Center art gallery, Harness Creek overlook,
    South River overlook, woodlands

Jewel-like Quiet Waters Park provides a 336-acre haven for waterfowl, eagles, pileated woodpeckers, great horned owls, bluebirds, foxes, and deer—and a tranquil loop perfect for a short bicycle-trip-cum-picnic. Once a farm, in 1986 this tract was scheduled to be bulldozed for 250 new homes. But neighbors objected and persuaded the county to purchase the land and turn it into a very elegant park, with gazebos, picnic pavilions, a skating rink, footpaths, and a bike trail.

The park is located off Forest Drive on Hillsmere Drive in Annapolis. It is open from dawn to dusk, except Tuesdays, and admission is charged for cars. The tour begins at the first parking lot after the entrance, adjacent to the Red Maple Pavilion.

0.0 *From the parking lot, go past the Sassafras Pavilion and enter the bike path, which winds through thick woods, curving gently.*

0.8 *Follow the bike path, which curves left. Bikes are not allowed on the footpath, which goes straight ahead.*

1.0 *At the Dogwood Pavilion, turn left again.*

1.1 *The Blue Heron Center, to your left, just past the parking lot, is used for weddings and parties.*

A gazebo overlooks the South River in Quiet Waters Park.

1.2   The Visitor Center on your left has a gallery with frequently changing shows by local artists, as well as rest rooms and a snack bar.

1.3   Just past the Visitor Center, the bike path curves to the right, going down and then up a hill.

1.5   By the Holly Pavilion, the path curves right, back into the woods.

1.7   Stop at the overlook high above quiet Harness Creek, a favorite anchorage for sailboats. After the overlook, the path curves left, then right again.

2.3   Turn right, following the sign to the South River Overlook.

2.6   Park your bike in the rack near the gazebo and drink in a spectacular view of the mouth of the South River and the seemingly endless Chesapeake Bay. Steps or a footpath take you down level with the river. After your visit, reverse direction on the bike path.

2.9   Turn right on the bike path, which goes through a meadow on the edge of the woods and curves back to the main park road.

3.5   Turn right on the park road and follow it up the hill to the ice rink.

3.7   Just past the ice rink on your left, turn right onto the bike path, which goes through a narrow strip of park with a fence on one side and a fitness course on the other.

4.6   The path skirts some wetlands, then crosses the park road.

4.9   After crossing the road, the path re-enters the woods.

5.1   Just past the maintenance compound to your left, take the exit to Sassafras Pavilion.

5.2   Return to the parking lot.

Bicycle Repair Service

Capitol Bicycle Center
25 Old Solomons Island Road, Annapolis
410-266-5510
No rentals

GREATER
FREDERICK AREA

11
A Not-for-Loafers Sugarloaf Tour

Location: *Frederick County, near the Montgomery County line*
Terrain: *Hilly*
Road conditions: *Some dirt and gravel roads, light traffic*
Distance: *19.2 miles, with a 15.9-mile alternate route*
Highlights: *Sugarloaf Mountain Park, Lily Pons Water Gardens, the Monacacy River*

One day in 1902 a wealthy young man named Gordon Strong bicycled from Washington, DC toward Frederick, Maryland. On his way he caught a glimpse of Sugarloaf Mountain, and it was love at first sight. Strong eventually bought the mountain and built a home, Stronghold, on its slopes. Stronghold now rents out for weddings, and the mountain is the centerpiece of a 3,000-acre park run by the Stronghold Foundation and open to the public since 1926. One visitor, President Franklin Delano Roosevelt, coveted the place and tried to get Strong to sell it to the government for a summer White House. Strong declined but graciously told FDR about the site in the nearby Catoctin Mountains that later became Shangri-La and, still later, Camp David.

Sugarloaf rises dramatically from the rather flat Monacacy Valley to 1,280 feet. The tallest thing around, it was used as a watchtower and signal station by Union troops monitoring Lee's progress toward Antietam.

This tour does not require you to bike all the way from Washington or even to climb the mountain, although old ladies and toddlers walk up to the summit on the stone steps regularly. If you do want to climb it, bike or drive to the second parking lot on the mountain *before* you start the bike tour. It's an easy climb from that point, but after this rigorous ride around the base of Sugarloaf you'll probably be too tired to attempt the climb. The tour begins in the parking lot at the base of the mountain.

0.0 From the parking lot, follow the road that hugs the base of the mountain, Comus Road, heading west.

0.5 Turn right on Mount Ephraim Road, which is hard-packed dirt and gravel.

0.9 An old yellow schoolhouse and white-clapboarded Bell's Chapel form a small settlement to your left. Then the road reenters the wooded park, traveling up and down small hills through woods filled with mountain laurel.

Watch for deer heading down toward Furnace Branch or Bear Branch to drink.

2.5 Mount Ephraim Road veers to the left, crossing Bear Branch.

After a rainstorm, there may be water on the road. Equestrian trails criss-cross the road in this area, so watch for horses.

3.8 Just after you pass the intersection with Stewart Hill Road, Mount Ephraim Road becomes paved and crosses Bennett Creek on a concrete bridge.

4.2 At the intersection of Bear Branch Road stands a small settlement marked by an abandoned nineteenth-century grocery store, a few houses, and several formidable-looking but friendly dogs. Turn left and follow Bear Branch Road down a hill.

4.3 Turn left on Park Mills Road. Watch for traffic. (There is not much, but more than on the roads previously traveled.)

5.7 Turn right on Lily Pons Road.

6.5 Turn right into Lily Pons Water Gardens.

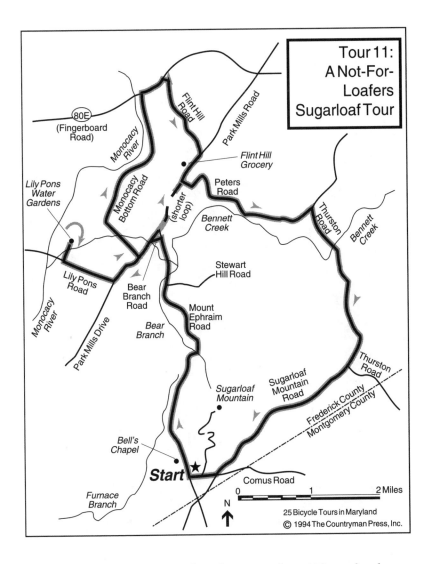

Tour 11: A Not-For-Loafers Sugarloaf Tour

80E (Fingerboard Road)

Flint Hill Road

Park Mills Road

Monocacy River

Flint Hill Grocery

Monocacy Bottom Road

Peters Road

Lily Pons Water Gardens

(shorter loop)

Bennett Creek

Thurston Road

Bennett Creek

Lily Pons Road

Monocacy River

Bear Branch Road

Stewart Hill Road

Mount Ephraim Road

Park Mills Drive

Bear Branch

Sugarloaf Mountain

Sugarloaf Mountain Road

Thurston Road

Frederick County Montgomery County

Bell's Chapel

Start

Comus Road

Furnace Branch

0   1   2 Miles

N

25 Bicycle Tours in Maryland
© 1994 The Countryman Press, Inc.

This 360-acre aqua-farm has more than 400 ponds where crops of goldfish and water lilies are raised. The enterprise was originally known as Three Springs Fishery, but when its mail-order business became substantial, in the 1930s,

A cyclist explores an abandoned log cabin on a country road near Sugarloaf Mountain.

the government agreed to give it its own post office. A punning opera buff suggested naming it after the then-reigning diva of the Metropolitan Opera, and Miss Pons graciously agreed. Visitors are free to wander around the ponds, but there are better views of the fish in the tanks in back of the store. Rest rooms and a soda machine are available.

6.6 Exit the fish farm and go back to the intersection of Lily Pons Road and Park Mills Road.

7.4 Turn left on Park Mills Road.

7.8 Turn left on Monacacy Bottom Road, which is unmarked. A white house stands on the corner. (If the weather has been very rainy, or if you really can't stand gravel roads, continue on Park Mills Road to the intersection with Peters Road, a distance of 1.5 miles. Pick up the main tour at the 12.6-mile point.)

Go slowly on Monacacy Bottom Road, which is gravel. You may want to picnic by the ponds that are part of Lily Pons Water Gardens.

8.6 The road comes to a branch of the Monacacy River.

This popular fishing spot is surrounded by woods filled with bluebonnets. In wet seasons, the road is underwater—but, usually, not much water. It's possible and quite pleasant to walk your bike across. People with pick-up trucks may also come to your rescue. Once across, follow Monacacy Bottom Road to the right, up a hill and through a rural residential neighborhood. Once over the crest, you can coast downhill for a stretch along the broad, flat main branch of the Monacacy, which means "stream of big bends." Native Americans used the Monacacy as part of a canoe trail from New York State to North Carolina.

10.5 Turn right on Fingerboard Road (MD 80E).

10.9 Turn right on Flinthill Road, which winds up a hill, then along a creek lined with mayapples.

12.1 Turn right on Park Mills Road, along a ridge with good views.

12.4 Flint Hill Grocery, the only store on the route, is on your right.

12.6 At the bottom of a hill, turn left on Peters Road. This is a narrow, hard-packed dirt and gravel road through a rural, wooded area with a sheep farm. Once it crests a hill, the road follows Bennett Creek.

15.0 Turn right on Thurston Road, which is busier and paved.

17.3 Turn right on Sugarloaf Mountain Road, which climbs a hill through woods and farmland.

18.2 Sugarloaf Mountain Road becomes a dirt and gravel road.

19.0 Sugarloaf Mountain Road ends at Comus Road. Turn right on Comus Road.

19.2 Return to parking lot.

Bicycle Repair Service

Frederick Bicycle Sales and Service
1216 West Patrick Street, Frederick
301-663-4452
No rentals

12
A Battlefield–Winery Loop

Location: *Washington County*
Terrain: *Rolling; flat on the Chesapeake & Ohio Canal towpath*
Road conditions: *Paved country roads and one stretch of dirt road with light traffic; unpaved towpath with some rough spots*
Distance: *21.2 miles*
Highlights: *Antietam Battlefield, the Ziem Winery, the Chesapeake & Ohio Canal*

On September 17, 1862, Union and Confederate troops clashed near Sharpsburg, Maryland. By late afternoon more than 23,000 of them were dead—making that day the bloodiest of the Civil War.

This tour begins at the Visitor Center of Antietam National Battlefield, where an excellent film interprets the historic battle. It travels through part of the battlefield, then exits the park and continues on country roads to the Ziem Vineyards for a tasting tour of Maryland's westernmost winery. More country roads lead to the Chesapeake & Ohio Canal towpath, between the mostly dried-up canal and the Potomac River. Leaving the towpath, the tour travels through farmland to the nineteenth-century town of Sharpsburg, then returns to the Visitor Center.

The Antietam National Battlefield Visitor Center is on MD 65 just north of the intersection with MD 34. Admission to the battlefield is free, but there is an admission charge to the Visitor Center.

0.0   Exit the Visitor Center parking lot and turn right.

> Just across the road is the Dunker Church, focal point of repeated clashes during the battle. Destroyed by a storm

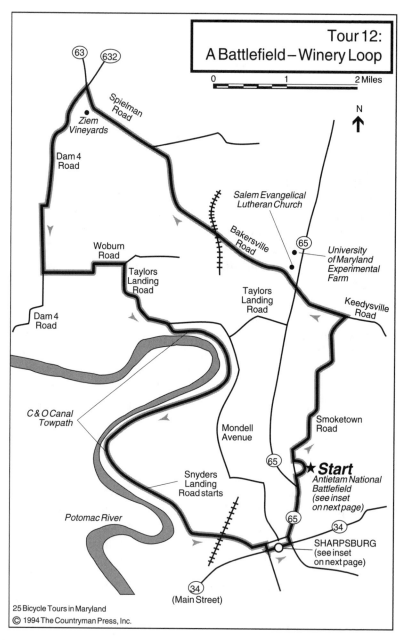

Tour 12:
A Battlefield – Winery Loop

0   1   2 Miles

N

63   632

Spielman Road

Ziem Vineyards

Dam 4 Road

Salem Evangelical Lutheran Church

Bakersville Road

65

Woburn Road

Taylors Landing Road

Taylors Landing Road

University of Maryland Experimental Farm

Keedysville Road

Dam 4 Road

C & O Canal Towpath

Smoketown Road

Mondell Avenue

65

★ *Start*
Antietam National Battlefield (see inset on next page)

Snyders Landing Road starts

Potomac River

65

34

SHARPSBURG *(see inset on next page)*

34
(Main Street)

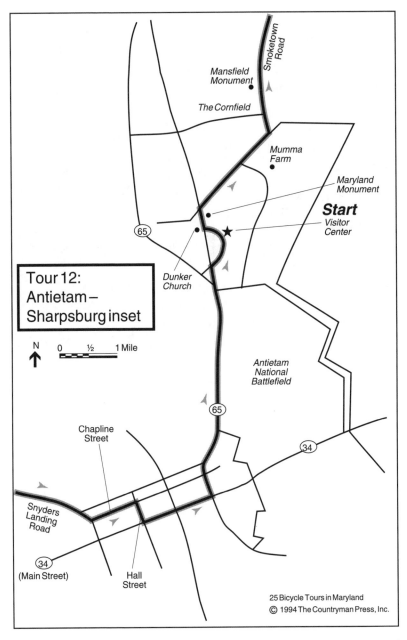

Smoketown Road

Mansfield Monument

The Cornfield

Mumma Farm

Maryland Monument

Start

Visitor Center

(65)

Tour 12: Antietam– Sharpsburg inset

Dunker Church

N

0   ½   1 Mile

Antietam National Battlefield

(65)

Chapline Street

(34)

Snyders Landing Road

(34) (Main Street)

Hall Street

25 Bicycle Tours in Maryland
© 1994 The Countryman Press, Inc.

A cyclist pedals past the monument to Union General Joseph K. Mansfield, killed at the Battle of Antietam.

in 1921, it was rebuilt in the original style in 1962.

0.1 *In front of the Maryland Monument, erected in memory of Marylanders who died here, bear right on Smoketown Road.*

On your left, in the cornfield of the Miller farm, more fighting took place than anywhere else on the battlefield. According to Union General Joseph Hooker, "every stalk of corn in the northern and greater part of the field was cut as closely as could have been done with a knife, and the slain lay in rows precisely as they had stood in their ranks a few moments before." At right is the Mumma farm, whose now-restored buildings were burned by Confederates to prevent their use by Union troops.

0.8   *At left stands a monument to Union General Joseph Mansfield.*

Beyond the Mansfield Monument, Smoketown Road turns into a hard-packed dirt road.

2.4   *Turn left on Keedysville Road.*

At right is the University of Maryland Experimental Farm.

3.2   *After crossing MD 65, Keedysville Road becomes Bakersville Road and passes Salem Evangelical Lutheran Church, to your right, built in 1854.*

4.6   *After passing under a railroad bridge, Bakersville Road becomes a series of roller-coaster hills.*

6.3   *At the V, bear left on Spielman Road.*

7.4   *Turn left into Ziem Vineyards.*

Winemaker Robert Ziem, a former NASA chemist, personally conducts some tours of the winery, which is housed in a 200-year-old barn. In the tasting room, Ziem's five reds and four whites are offered for sampling and purchase. All are made from the grapes grown at the vineyards.

7.8   *Exiting the vineyard grounds, turn left and continue on Speilman Road.*

8.0   *Bear left at the V and then turn left on Dam No. 4 Road.*

10.8   *Turn left on Woburn Road, which leads past some suburban-type houses and up a modest hill.*

12.1   *Turn right on Taylor's Landing Road for a delightful downhill swoop to the Potomac River and the Chesapeake & Ohio Canal towpath.*

13.4   *Enter the towpath and turn left.*

In spring, look for bluebonnets, mayapples, lilies-of-the-valley, and violets along the path. In all seasons you may need to walk your bike around boulders and other rough spots. The canal, and the towpath, follow the river in a wide horseshoe bend. There are some good places for a swim in the Potomac in this stretch.

18.0 *Cross the canal on a footbridge and follow Snyders Landing Road, which winds uphill, through verdant woods into a farming area.*

18.9 *Snyders Landing Road passes under a railroad bridge.*

19.4 *Turn left on Chapline Street.*

19.6 *Turn right on Hall Street.*

19.8 *Turn left on Main Street.*

The Jacob Rohrbach house, on the southeast corner of Hall and Main, is now a bed-and-breakfast. Its name reflects the fact that many of the original settlers of this area were German. A Union sympathizer like most of his fellow townspeople, Jacob Rohrbach was killed defending his home from Confederate troops. Like the Rohrbach home, most of the brick houses in this nineteenth-century town are built close to the road.

20.2 *Turn left on MD 65.*

21.2 *Turn right into the Visitor Center.*

Bicycle Repair Services

Hub City Cycle Center
35 North Prospect, Hagerstown
301-797-9877

Potomac Pushbikes
11 East Potomac Street, Williamsport
301-582-4747
Rentals

Accommodations

Jacob Rohrbach Inn
138 West Main Street, Sharpsburg, MD 21782
301-432-5079

Inn at Antietam
220 East Main Street, Sharpsburg, MD 21782
301-432-6601

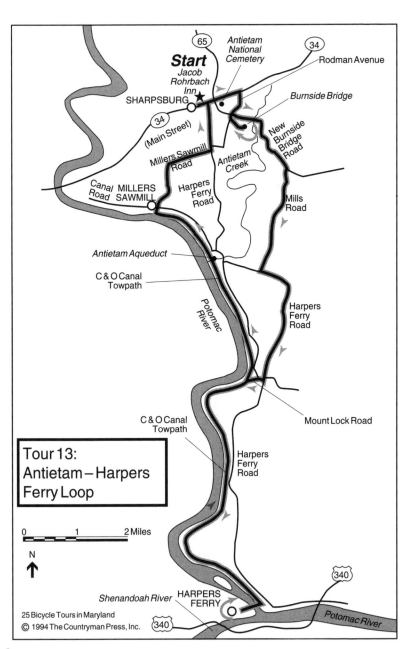

65

Start
Jacob
Rohrbach
Inn
SHARPSBURG ★

Antietam
National
Cemetery

34

Rodman Avenue

Burnside Bridge

34

(Main Street)

Millers Sawmill
Road

New
Burnside
Bridge
Road

Antietam
Creek

Canal
Road

MILLERS
SAWMILL

Harpers
Ferry
Road

Mills
Road

Antietam Aqueduct

C & O Canal
Towpath

Potomac
River

Harpers
Ferry
Road

Harpers
Ferry
Road

Mount Lock Road

C & O Canal
Towpath

Tour 13:
Antietam – Harpers
Ferry Loop

0   1   2 Miles

N

340

Shenandoah River   HARPERS
FERRY

340

Potomac River

25 Bicycle Tours in Maryland
© 1994 The Countryman Press, Inc.

100

13
Antietam–Harpers Ferry Loop

Location: *Washington County*
Terrain: *Moderately hilly; flat on towpath*
Road conditions: *Country roads with light traffic; Chesapeake &
Ohio Canal towpath, which is unpaved but easily cycled*
Distance: *27.2 miles*
Highlights: *Antietam National Cemetery, Antietam Battlefield, the
Burnside Bridge, the Chesapeake & Ohio Canal, Harpers Ferry,
West Virginia*

In a sense, the Civil War began not at Fort Sumter but at Harpers Ferry,
where John Brown fired the shots heard round the world. And, although the war didn't end at Antietam, the battle really sealed the fate
of the Confederacy. Lee's failure to win a decisive victory and carry the
war onto Northern turf convinced the European powers not to inter-
vene on the South's behalf.

This tour, a good second-day follow-up to the Antietam-Ziem Winery loop (see tour 12), begins at the Jacob Rohrbach Inn on Main Street
in Sharpsburg and passes the national cemetery where some 5,000
federal soldiers—almost half of them unknowns—were laid to rest. The
tour then enters the battlefield park and visits the Burnside Bridge,
turning point of the battle. Leaving the park, it follows country roads
to the Chesapeake & Ohio Canal towpath, which leads along the
Potomac River toward Harpers Ferry. That historic town is accessible
from the towpath via a pedestrian bridge across the Potomac. The
return trip doubles back along the towpath and then enters Sharpsburg
by a different route.

0.0   *Leave the Jacob Rohrbach Inn, whose original owner was killed defending his home from Confederate raiders during the Battle of Antietam. If you are not staying at the inn, park on Main Street (MD 34) and proceed east.*

0.5   *To your right is Antietam National Cemetery.*

Most of the Confederate dead are buried elsewhere—some in local churchyards.

0.9   *Turn right on Rodman Avenue (unmarked) into the battlefield park. Follow the road up a hill and down again. Turn left in front of a farmhouse that was there since before the battle, following signs to the Burnside Bridge.*

1.9   *Using the handicapped-access route, bike directly to the historic bridge over Antietam Creek. Otherwise, you will have to bike up a steep hill to the parking lot and walk down a flight of steps.*

From about 9:30 AM on September 17, 1862, Federal troops led by Gen. Ambrose E. Burnside tried to cross this stone arch bridge across Antietam Creek, but were continually driven back by about 400 Georgians. By 1 PM they succeeded, and by late afternoon they had driven the Georgians almost back to Sharpsburg. But then fresh Confederate troops arrived from Harpers Ferry and drove Burnside back to the heights above the bridge that now bears his name. Indecisive as this sounds, it meant that the Battle of Antietam was over. The next day, Lee began withdrawing his forces across the Potomac. Today the hard-fought bridge is a popular spot for picnics and for launching canoes on Antietam Creek. After viewing the bridge, turn back to the intersection by the old farmhouse.

2.4   *Walk your bike down the grassy bank and turn right on New Burnside Bridge Road, which climbs some winding hills.*

4.3   *Turn right on Mills Road.*

Visitors stroll the streets of historic Harpers Ferry, site of John Brown's raid.

6.0 *Turn left on Harpers Ferry Road.*

8.3 *Turn right on Mount Lock Road and follow it downhill to the towpath.*

8.5 *Enter the Chesapeake & Ohio Canal towpath and turn left.*

In the days when the canal was operational—from the 1830s through the 1870s—two mules, led by a mule driver, would tread this path for each boat. Average speed was between two and three miles per hour.

12.4 *To your left are the ruins of a lock tender's house, which was part of the pay for the job.*

14.1 *Lock your bike and climb the steps to an old truss railroad bridge, which has a safe wooden walkway across the Potomac to Harpers Ferry. Do not use the upstream girder bridge, which still carries trains.*

Stop at the Visitors Center on Shenandoah Street and pick up a map for a self-guided tour. The arsenal—captured in 1959 by abolitionist John Brown and recaptured by then US Army officer Robert E. Lee after a bloody fight—is right in front of you after you leave the bridge. Harpers Ferry also has restaurants and rest rooms. After visiting Harpers Ferry, re-cross the bridge and turn left on the towpath.

22.8 *The towpath crosses Antietam Aqueduct, which carried the canal across Antietam Creek. It's best to walk your bike across because the grass conceals dangerous crevices.*

24.2 *Exit the towpath, walking your bike across the dry, grass-covered canal and across the frontage road. Head up Millers Sawmill Road, which travels through a small settlement and winds up and down some roller-coaster hills.*

25.9 *Turn left on Harpers Ferry Road, which leads into Sharpsburg.*

27.0 Turn left on Main Street.

27.2 Arrive back at Jacob Rohrbach Inn.

Bicycle Repair Services

Hub City Cycle Center
35 North Prospect, Hagerstown
301-797-9877
No rentals

Potomac Pushbikes
11 East Potomac Street, Williamsport
301-582-4747
Rentals

Accommodations

Jacob Rohrbach Inn
138 West Main Street, Sharpsburg, MD 21782
301-432-5079

Inn at Antietam
220 East Main Street, Sharpsburg, MD 21782
301-432-6601

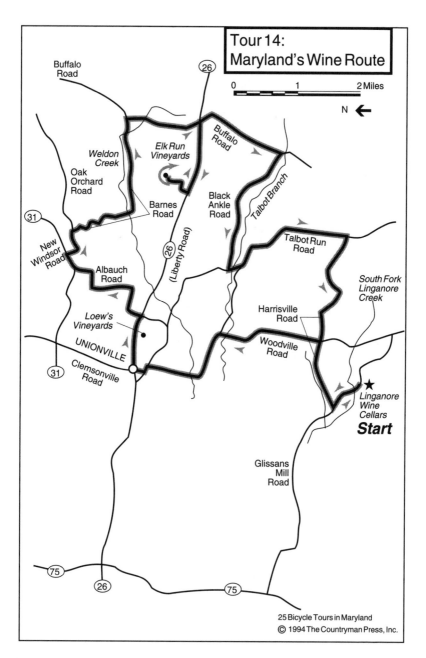

Tour 14:
Maryland's Wine Route

0   1   2 Miles

N ←

Buffalo Road

26

Elk Run Vineyards

Buffalo Road

Weldon Creek

Oak Orchard Road

Barnes Road

Black Ankle Road

Talbot Branch

31

New Windsor Road

(Liberty Road)

26

Albauch Road

Talbot Run Road

South Fork Linganore Creek

Loew's Vineyards

Harrisville Road

UNIONVILLE

Woodville Road

31

Clemsonville Road

★ Linganore Wine Cellars

Start

Glissans Mill Road

75

26

75

25 Bicycle Tours in Maryland
© 1994 The Countryman Press, Inc.

14
Maryland's Wine Route

Location: Frederick County
Terrain: Moderately hilly
Road conditions: Paved country roads, most with light traffic
Distance: 23 miles
Highlights: Linganore Winecellars, Loew Vineyards, Elk Run Vineyards

Early Marylanders made wine from whatever berries and fruits they had handy. And, in the seventeenth century, Lord Baltimore tried to import European vines, but they died on the long sea voyage. Catawba grapes were successfully grown and made into wine for many years, but European-style winemaking from vinifera grapes began when a *Baltimore Sun* correspondent smuggled cuttings of vines out of France during the Second World War. The state now has about a dozen wineries, producing 600,000 bottles a year with total sales of more than $2.5 million.

This tour loops through the rolling farmland of Frederick County near Mount Airy—an area of weathered red barns and small, lively streams—and visits three wineries that offer tours and tastings. It begins at Linganore Winecellars at 13601 Glissans Mill Road in Mount Airy. To reach the winery, take exit 62 from I-70 and head north on MD 75 to Glissans Mill Road. Take Glissans Mill Road east to the winery, which has a large parking lot, picnic grounds, and a wide variety of wines—from dandelion wine to more conventional types.

0.0   From the parking lot, a dirt drive leads down a hill, past a pond.

0.3   Exit the vineyard grounds, turning left on Glissans Mill Road, a country road lined with farms and cattle ranches.

0.8   After crossing a narrow brook, turn right on Harrisville Road, which is unmarked and runs just south of another stream.

1.8   Turn left on Woodville Road, which rolls and winds through farmland and suburban-type houses.

5.0   At the fork in the gingerbread village of Unionville, bear right on Clemsonville Road.

5.2   At the intersection with Liberty Road (MD 26), turn right.

5.8   At the sign, turn right into Loew Vineyards.

5.9   Leave your bike outside the tasting room and sample some of the offerings of this 4-acre vineyard.

The vineyard's owner is from Austria. Among the wines available are Chardonnay, Seyval, and Cabernet Sauvignon.

6.0   Exit the vineyard grounds and turn right on Liberty Road.

6.2   Crossing the road carefully, turn left on Albaugh Road, a hard-packed gravel road that turns right and leads up and down a series of roller-coaster hills.

7.9   Turn right on New Windsor Road (MD 31).

8.1   Turn right on Oak Orchard Road.

8.4   Turn right on Barnes Road, which goes down a hill into a ferny, wooded dell and winds along Weldon Creek.

10.8 Barnes Road ends. Turn right on Buffalo Road, which goes up a hill through woods.

Elk Run Vineyards offers wine tastings in a restored stone tavern.

11.9   *Turn right on Liberty Road (MD 26).*

12.9   *Turn right into Elk Run Vineyards, whose tasting room is housed in the summer kitchen of a c. 1750 stone house that served as a tavern for travelers between Baltimore and Frederick—Liberty Tavern on Liberty Road.*

> Some of Elk Run's best, prize-winning wines are named for the tavern: Liberty Tavern Reserve Chardonnay and Liberty Tavern Reserve Cabernet Sauvignon. The winery also produces an excellent Gewurztraminer.

13.0   *After your tour, leave the winery grounds and turn left on Liberty Road, doubling back.*

14.0   *Turn right on Buffalo Road, which leads downhill, through woods thick with goldfinches, past a lumber mill.*

15.4   *Make a sharp right onto Black Ankle Road, which is unmarked. This narrow road leads first through woods, along gurgling Talbot Branch, then emerges by fields grazed by Black Angus cattle.*

17.5   *At the stop sign, turn left.*

17.6   *Turn left again on Talbot Run Road.*

19.6   *Turn left on Harrisville Road.*

22.4   *Turn left on Glissans Mill Road.*

23.0   *Re-enter Linganore Winecellars grounds.*

Bicycle Repair Service

Mount Airy Bicycles
4540 Old National Pike, Mount Airy
301-831-5151
Rentals

NORTHEAST
MARYLAND

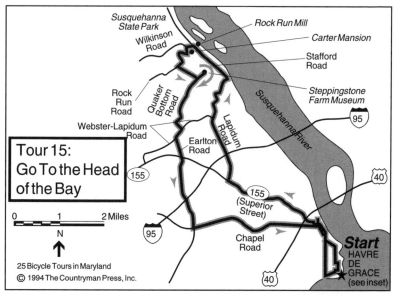

Tour 15:
Go To the Head
of the Bay

Susquehanna
State Park

Rock Run Mill

Carter Mansion

Wilkinson
Road

Stafford
Road

Steppingstone
Farm Museum

Rock
Run
Road

Quaker Bottom Road

Webster-Lapidum
Road

Lapidum Road

Susquehanna River

95

Earlton
Road

155

155
(Superior
Street)

40

Chapel
Road

95

40

Start
HAVRE
DE
GRACE
(see inset)

0   1   2 Miles
N

25 Bicycle Tours in Maryland
© 1994 The Countryman Press, Inc.

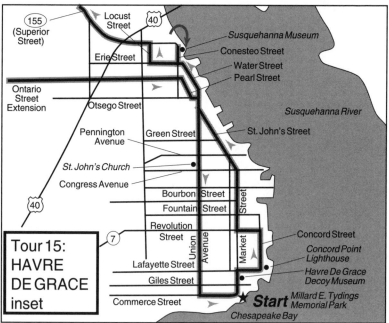

155
(Superior
Street)

Locust
Street

40

Susquehanna Museum

Conesteo Street

Water Street

Pearl Street

Erie Street

Ontario
Street
Extension

Otsego Street

Susquehanna River

Pennington
Avenue

Green Street

St. John's Street

St. John's Church

Congress Avenue

40

Bourbon Street

Fountain Street

Market Street

Revolution
Street

Union Avenue

Concord Street

Concord Point
Lighthouse

7

Lafayette Street

Tour 15:
HAVRE
DE GRACE
inset

Giles Street

Havre De Grace
Decoy Museum

Commerce Street

Start   Millard E. Tydings
Memorial Park

Chesapeake Bay

15

Go to the Head of the Bay

Location: *Havre de Grace and surrounding Harford County*
Terrain: *Hilly*
Road conditions: *Paved roads, most with light traffic*
Distance: *17.8 miles*
Highlights: *Historic Havre de Grace, the Concord Point Lighthouse, the Susquehanna & Tidewater Canal and Lockhouse, Susquehanna State Park, the Steppingstone Museum*

Lafayette was not only here—he named the place: harbor of grace. Don't try pronouncing it as Lafayette would have, however. Today, it's "hay-ver-dee-grayce," but still a graceful and gracious town at the head of Chesapeake Bay and the mouth of the Susquehanna River. A ferry ran across the Susquehanna from here in the early eighteenth century, and taverns and inns met the needs of travelers going to and from Philadelphia. Later modes of transport, including a canal and the railroad, also enriched the town, economically as well as historically.

This tour begins on the Havre de Grace waterfront (in Tydings Memorial Park at the foot of Union Avenue), visits the old canal lockhouse, travels into the country and along the Susquehanna River, and returns to the starting point via the historic residential district.

0.0   Exit the park, named for favorite son Senator Millard Tydings, and turn right, continuing along the waterfront on Commerce Street, which immediately turns right and becomes Market Street.

0.1 *At right, at Giles and Market Streets, is the Havre de Grace Decoy Museum.*

> The museum celebrates a local folk art. There is an admission fee.

0.2 *Turn right on Lafayette Street and ride three blocks to the Concord Point Lighthouse, the oldest continuously operating lighthouse in the state.*

> The 36-foot granite tower, begun in 1826, originally used whale-oil lamps with tin reflectors to warn sailors off the hazardous shoals where the river flows into the bay. It was electrified in 1920. John O'Neill, an Irish immigrant, was the first keeper—a post earned as a reward for heroism on the site during the War of 1812. From a small fort located here, O'Neill fired a single cannon at the British in a vain attempt to stave off an invasion. He was wounded, captured, and scheduled for hanging, but his daughter obtained his release from the British commander, Admiral Cockburn (who later burned the White House). The post was almost hereditary: O'Neills held the job, with only an occasional hiatus, until 1919. The decommissioned lighthouse is now run by a volunteer group, which is in the process of restoring the lighthouse keeper's home across the street. Visitors may climb the winding staircase of the lighthouse on weekend afternoons from May to October. Admission is free.

0.3 *Exiting the lighthouse, turn right on Concord Street, which runs along the waterfront.*

0.5 *Turn left on Revolution Street.*

0.6 *Turn right on Market Street, which has several antique shops.*

1.0 *Bear left on St. John Street.*

1.4 *St. John Street dead-ends at Union Avenue. Bear right.*

1.5   *After crossing Otsego Street, continue straight, on Water Street.*

At 654 Water Street, across from a rather industrial-looking waterfront, stands Price's Seafood Restaurant, which has excellent crab cakes and soft crabs at reasonable prices.

1.7   *Turn left on Erie Street.*

1.9   *Turn right on Conesteo Street to the Susquehanna Museum, in the lock tender's house at the southern terminus of the Susquehanna & Tidewater Canal.*

Opened in 1839, the Susquehanna & Tidewater Canal ran 45 miles upriver, into the rich farmland of Pennsylvania. After a heyday in the 1860s, the canal gradually declined in importance, a victim of competition from the railroads. The lock is still visible, and volunteers conduct tours of the lock tender's house. The museum is open Sunday afternoons from April through October. Admission is free.

Unfortunately, only a small section of the towpath used by the mules is still there, adjacent to the museum. Volunteers dream of resurrecting it one day. Until then, bicyclists have to continue this tour by road. After touring the museum, retrace your path to Erie Street and turn right.

2.3   *Turn right on Locust Street.*

2.4   *Turn left on Superior Street, which becomes MD 155. This is a busy road with a shoulder. It leaves Havre de Grace and climbs a long, winding hill.*

4.4   *Turn right on Lapidum Road, which, after crossing over I-95, turns into a country road that travels mainly downhill.*

6.2   *Lapidum Road enters Susquehanna State Park.*

7.0   *Lapidum Road ends at the Susquehanna River.*

There is a boat launch here, and you can see traces of the

Rock Run Mill, built near the end of the 18th century on the Susquehanna River, has been restored.

old canal and of the railroad tracks that displaced it. Turn left on Stafford Road, which runs along the wide, island-strewn river.

8.0   *On your right is the restored Rock Run Mill, built near the end of the eighteenth century.*

Corn is ground at the mill for visitors on summer weekends. Take time to stroll along the river and view the remains of a bridge that once crossed it here. Adjacent to the mill is a restored canal tollhouse with an exhibit on the ecology of the river and the Chesapeake Bay.

8.1   *Turn left on Rock Run Road.*

8.2   *The Carter Mansion (left), a magnificent stone house built in 1804 by one of the owners of the mill, is open on summer weekends.*

8.4   *At the intersection with Wilkinson Road, keep left on Rock Run Road, which winds uphill, along a stream.*

8.9   *Turn left on Quaker Bottom Road and continue uphill.*

9.5   *Turn left onto the grounds of the Steppingstone Museum.*

The museum is dedicated to preserving the rural arts and crafts of the period from 1880 to 1920. A once-working farm, it includes a blacksmith's shop, a cooper shop, a potter's shed, a dairy, and many other buildings, with demonstrations in each. The museum is open weekends from May through the first weekend in October, and admission is charged. After touring the museum and exiting the grounds, continue straight on Quaker Bottom Road.

11.5 *Turn right on Webster-Lapidum Road.*

11.7 *Turn left on Earlton Road.*

13.6 *Turn left on Chapel Road.*

15.9 *Chapel Road crosses the railroad tracks and becomes Ontario Street Extension.*

16.0 *Cross US 40 at the light. Fast-food restaurants are available here. Continue on Ontario Street through an old residential neighborhood of Havre de Grace.*

16.4 *Ontario Street ends. Turn right on Pearl Street.*

16.5 *Turn left on Ostego Street.*

16.6 *Turn right on Union Avenue, lined with antique shops in this area. Then the shops give way to grand old homes.*

16.8 **On the northwest corner, at the intersection of Union and Green, stands the stands the Aveilhe-Goldsborough house.**

The Aveilhe-Goldsborough house was built by a French émigré in 1801 in the French style. Note the hipped slate roof. Just across Green Street, on both sides of Union Avenue, are brick homes built by members of the Hopkins family during the canal era.

On the northwest corner of Union and Pennington stands the Seneca Mansion, a grand frame Victorian built by a former city mayor. The 22-room structure is an exuberant hodgepodge of turrets, domes, dormers, and bays.

One block farther, at the intersection with Congress Street, stands St. John's Church, built in 1809 in Flemish bond. The Methodist Church, diagonally across the street and built almost a century later, provides a striking contrast to simple St. John's. The imposing church, constructed on local granite, features elaborate arches filled with stained glass windows. Just to the south of the church are two frame houses, built in a combination of the Queen Anne and Stick styles in the 1880s by Arthur Vosbury—one for his daughter and one for his son.

At the southwest corner of Bourbon and Union is the Spencer-Silver Mansion, now a bed-and-breakfast inn. This high Victorian stone house was built in 1896 by John Spencer, a foundry owner, and later purchased by Charles Silver, who owned a cannery. At 301 South Union, at the intersection with Fountain Street, stands the Vandiver Inn, a very large Queen Anne cottage with five chimneys. The house was built in 1886 by Murray Vandiver, then mayor of Havre de Grace. In addition to accommodations, the inn also offers excellent dinners.

17.7 Turn left on Commerce Street.

17.8 Enter Tydings Park.

Bicycle Repair Service

Wheel Power
139 Thomas Street, Belair
410-879-8300

Accomodations

Vandiver Inn
301 South Union Avenue, Havre de Grace, MD 21078
410-939-5200

Spencer-Silver Mansion
200 South Union Avenue, Havre de Grace, MD 21078
410-939-1097

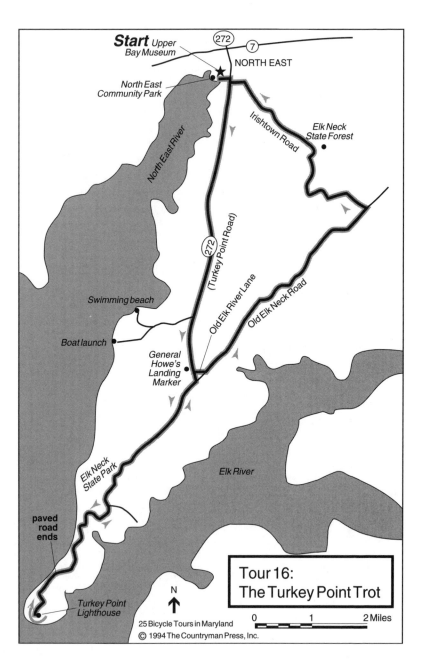

Start *Upper Bay Museum*

272

7

NORTH EAST

North East Community Park

North East River

Irishtown Road

Elk Neck State Forest

272

(Turkey Point Road)

Old Elk River Lane

Old Elk Neck Road

Swimming beach

Boat launch

General Howe's Landing Marker

Elk Neck State Park

Elk River

paved road ends

Turkey Point Lighthouse

N

Tour 16:
The Turkey Point Trot

25 Bicycle Tours in Maryland
© 1994 The Countryman Press, Inc.

0   1   2 Miles

120

16
Turkey Point

Location: *Cecil County*
Terrain: *Very hilly*
Road conditions: *Paved roads with seasonal traffic, one short dirt road*
Distance: 27.7 miles
Highlights: *The Upper Bay Museum, Elk Neck State Park, Turkey Point Lighthouse*

At the top end of Chesapeake Bay, the Northeast and Elk Rivers squeeze out a narrow V-shaped peninsula that is called Elk Neck but that ends at Turkey Point. This tour begins at the top of the neck, in North East, a small town equipped with seafood restaurants and antique shops just off I-95. The tour leads through wooded parkland to the lighthouse at Turkey Point, on a hundred-foot clay bluff at the confluence of the Elk River and Chesapeake Bay.

One of the chief differences between the Upper Bay region and the Bay country to the south is that the Upper Bay has more hills. For that reason—and because summer weekends bring heavy automobile traffic—this tour is recommended for brisker weather, perhaps during the fall foliage season.

Begin the tour at the Upper Bay Museum, located in North East Community Park, where there is ample parking. The museum, which charges admission, features decoys, boats, and other memorabilia related to fishing—particularly herring fishing—and duck hunting in the area. Note the ice-fishing house.

0.0   *Exit the community park onto Walnut Street.*

0.3   *Turn right on Main Street (MD 272), which becomes Turkey
Point Road and leads up and down a series of long, gradual
hills.*

5.7   *The paved shoulder ends and the road winds up a hill with
farmhouses on either side of the road.*

6.0   *At the top of the hill, look left for a view of farmland rolling
down to the Elk River.*

Three hundred British warships landed troops here on
August 27, 1877, under the command of General Howe.
The force marched up along the Elk River toward
Philadelphia and defeated Washington's troops at the
Battle of Brandywine on September 11.

6.5   *Turn right at the intersection for the park's swimming beach on
the Northeast River. Turn left to the boat launch area. To
continue the tour, go straight on Turkey Point Road, through
parkland covered with hardwoods, pines, ferns, and
rhododendron.*

Paths through the woods on the right lead to yellow-sand
beaches.

11.4   *Just past a nonpark, residential area, the paved road ends.
Follow a dirt-and-gravel park road that is rough in spots.*

12.3   *The road ends at the lighthouse, a 35-foot white tower built in
1834, on a rolling green lawn with picnic tables and views of
the Bay.*

Before the lighthouse was built, mariners, going back to
the time of Captain John Smith, used the white clay bluffs
below where the lighthouse now stands as a beacon.
Today, signs warn that erosion has made walking along
the cliff risky. After a rest stop at the lighthouse, reverse
direction and double back on Turkey Point Road.

Turkey Point Lighthouse towers above Chesapeake Bay
atop white clay cliffs.

18.7 Just past the small white church and the historical marker about General Howe's landing, on your left, turn right on Old Elk River Lane, and then make an immediate left onto Old Elk Neck Road, which has marginally fewer hills than Turkey Point Road and much less traffic.

23.3 Turn left on Irishtown Road, which skirts Elk Neck State Forest and runs through suburban subdivisions.

27.3 Cross MD 272 and ride on the sidewalk, against traffic for two blocks.

27.4 Turn left on Walnut Street.

27.7 Return to Upper Bay Museum.

Bicycle Repair Service

Wheel Power
139 Thomas Street, Belair
410-879-8300

Accommodations

North Bay Bed & Breakfast
9 Sunset Drive, North East, MD 21901
410-287-5948

Cabins and Campsites

Elk Neck State Park
4395 Turkey Point Road, North East, MD 21901
410-287-5333

SOUTHERN
MARYLAND

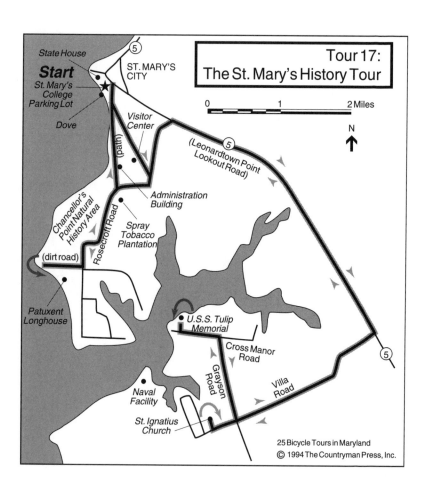

Tour 17:
The St. Mary's History Tour

State House
Start
St. Mary's College Parking Lot
Dove
ST. MARY'S CITY
5
Visitor Center
(path)
(Leonardtown Point Lookout Road)
5
N

0   1   2 Miles

Administration Building
Chancellor's Point Natural History Area
Rosecroft Road
Spray Tobacco Plantation
(dirt road)
Patuxent Longhouse
U.S.S. Tulip Memorial
Cross Manor Road
5
Naval Facility
Grayson Road
Villa Road
St. Ignatius Church

25 Bicycle Tours in Maryland
© 1994 The Countryman Press, Inc.

126

17
St. Mary's History Tour

Location: St. Mary's County
Terrain: Flat to rolling
Road conditions: Dirt and gravel walking and bike trails, park
  roads, highway with a wide shoulder
Distance: 13.8 miles
Highlights: Historic St. Mary's City, St. Ignatius Church, Cross
  Manor, the USS Tulip Memorial, a reconstructed Native American
  longhouse, the St. Mary's River

Maryland began in St. Mary's City, where Roman Catholics seeking religious freedom settled in 1634. Of course, Native Americans were there all along, and this tour also includes a visit to a reconstructed longhouse much like those lived in by the local tribes. When Maryland abolished freedom of worship in 1704, the Catholics of St. Mary's City fled downstream to the grounds of St. Inigoes Manor House—and so does the tour. The manor house is gone, but St. Ignatius Church, built in 1785 when Catholic churches were again legal, survives. The tour also stops at an eighteenth-century manor and a rarely visited memorial to seamen blown up in a Civil War disaster.

Start the tour on the campus of St. Mary's College, off MD 5, in the small parking lot just behind the reconstructed State House.

0.0   Enter the grounds of Historic St. Mary's City, walking your bike.

> To your right is an "ordinary," or inn, reconstructed on or near its original site. (If you want to enter this or any of the other structures, you must buy a ticket at the Visitor

The rebuilt "ordinary," or inn, in historic St. Mary's City, served visitors to Maryland's first capital.

Center. See below.) Straight ahead, down the hill, is the *Maryland Dove*, a reconstruction of the original square-rigger that brought the first colonists. The tour turns left, passing an archeological dig and following the path to the Visitor Center.

0.5   Exit the Visitor Center parking lot and turn left on Rosecroft Road.

1.0   Turn right onto MD 5, which has a wide shoulder and relatively little traffic.

3.1   Turn right on Villa Road, which goes up a small hill and through cornfields and woods.

4.3   Turn right on Grayson Road.

4.9   Bear left on Cross Manor Road, which is gravel.

Cross Manor (private but visible from the road) is a two-and-a-half-story dwelling once believed to be the oldest brick house in Maryland. It is now thought to have been built in 1765.

5.2 *Turn right and walk your bike down the grass right-of-way to the USS Tulip Memorial.*

This granite obelisk, erected in 1940, honors the 57 crewmen of a Civil War gunboat that blew up and sank near here en route to Washington for boiler repairs. Eight of the dead are buried here. Ten crewmen survived. After viewing the memorial, double back on Cross Manor Road.

5.6 *Turn right on Grayson's Road.*

6.2 *Turn right on Villa Road.*

6.6 *St. Ignatius Church is on your right.*

The church, built in 1785 and named for the founder of the Jesuit order, may be entered with a key obtained from the gatehouse of the naval facility just beyond it.

The Navy facility stands on the site of St. Inigoes Manor, whose Catholic owner could legally keep a chapel even after Maryland ended religious tolerance. Until the Revolution restored religious freedom, local Catholics worshiped there. After the Revolution, they built this church. Many Jesuits are buried in the adjacent churchyard. After your visit, double back on Villa Road.

8.0 *Turn left on MD 5, which climbs a slight hill.*

10.1 *Turn left on Rosecroft Road, which runs through cornfields and the St. Mary's City grounds.*

11.1 *On your left is the Godiah Spray Tobacco Plantation.*

The Plantation is a recreation of a 1660s tobacco farm. The cast of characters includes the Sprays, their children, and an indentured servant.

11.5 Turn right onto a hard-packed dirt road into the Chancellor's Point Natural History area.

11.8 On your right are picnic tables and paths to a beautiful beach on the St. Mary's River. On your left, across a field, is a recreation of a Patuxent Indian longhouse, constructed of sticks. Double back on the dirt road.

12.1 Turn left on Rosecroft Road.

12.7 Turn left into the driveway to the Administration Building, which leads to a path through woods and fields back to the Ordinary.

13.8 Arrive at the parking lot behind the Ordinary.

Bicycle Repair Service

Mike's Bike Shop
447-C Great Mills Road, Lexington Park
301-863-7887
No rentals

18
General Smallwood Country

Location: Charles County
Terrain: Rolling
Road conditions: Paved roads with light traffic
Distance: 26.5 miles
Highlights: Smallwood State Park, Old Durham Church, Nanjemoy
Creek, Chicamuxen Methodist Church

General William Smallwood probably saved George Washington at the
Battle of Long Island by covering the Continental Army's retreat to
Brooklyn. He lost 256 men in the process, but gained for Maryland the
title of "The Old Line State" for the way his troops held the line.
Smallwood served as Maryland's governor from 1785 to 1788, then
retired to his plantation, which is now a state park bearing his name.
The tour starts at this restored small-but-elegant plantation home and
travels through rolling farmland and woods to the Old Durham Church,
to which parishioner Smallwood once contributed 3,000 pounds of
tobacco for a new roof. After a picnic stop at a boat launching area and
fishing dock on picturesque Nanjemoy Creek, the route traverses swamp-
land and farms and loops back to the park.

To reach the park from the Washington Beltway, take MD 210 south
to the intersection with MD 225. Take MD 225 east to the intersection
with MD 224. Take MD 224 south to the park. There is an admission
charge, per car.

0.0 From the restored home and grave of General Smallwood, follow the signs to the park exit.

0.5 Continue up a small hill on Sweden Point Road.

0.8 Turn right on Mason Springs-Chicamuxen Road (MD 224), which goes down a hill and up another one.

1.4 Turn left on Smallwood Church Road, a country byway through woods and fields.

5.6 At the intersection, turn right on Mason Springs-Ironsides Road (MD 425) and follow it across MD 6.

7.0 To your left stands Old Durham Church, founded in 1692.

The rather plain, boxy brick church itself dates from 1732 and was restored 200 years later in honor of Smallwood, a vestryman. Another Smallwood connection: the bell tower is made of bricks from the ruins of the home of Smallwood's sister. A sundial in front of the church determined the time for beginning Sunday services, and the churchyard holds graves dating as far back as 1690.

8.2 Turn left on Friendship Landing Road.

This road leads to a public area on the banks of marshy Nanjemoy Creek, an excellent place to watch great blue herons.

9.8 After a stop by the creek, reverse direction along Friendship Landing Road.

11.4 Turn left on Ironsides-Riverside Road (MD 425).

12.0 At the bottom of a hill, turn right on Baptist Church Road.

13.7 After crossing a swamp bright with water lilies and loud with the croaking of frogs, the road climbs a small rise to the Nanjemoy Baptist Church, on your right.

In 1790 four men crossed the Potomac from Virginia to

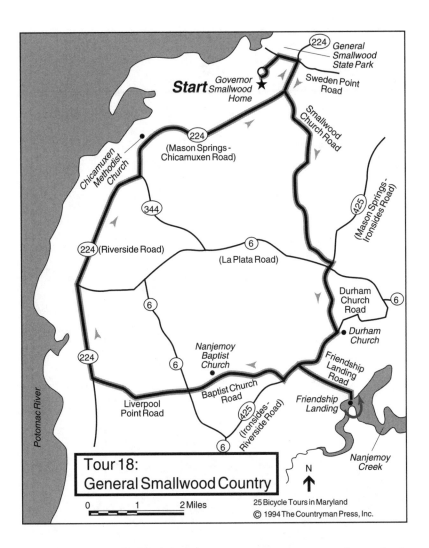

**Tour 18:
General Smallwood Country**

0   1   2 Miles

25 Bicycle Tours in Maryland
© 1994 The Countryman Press, Inc.

preach in this area, and five years later a church was built on this site. The present white-frame church dates from the nineteenth century.

14.2 After crossing MD 6, Baptist Church Road becomes Liverpool Point Road.

The time for services was set by this sundial at Old Durham Church.

15.8 The small store to your right sells snacks and cold drinks.

16.2 Turn right on Riverside Road (MD 224), which rolls up and down hills, crossing swamps and thick woods.

21.1 At the junction with MD 344, continue on MD 224, left onto what becomes Mason Springs–Chicamuxen Road.

22.5 The white frame Chicamuxen Methodist Church, to your left, served as headquarters for General Joseph Hooker.

Hooker's 12,000 troops camped along the Potomac near here from October 1861 until March 1862. The general's main claim to fame comes from his setting aside a red-light district in wartime Washington, thus lending his name to practitioners of the world's oldest profession.

25.7 Turn left on Sweden Point Road and follow it into Smallwood State Park.

26.5 Arrive at the parking lot for the Smallwood home.

Bicycle Repair Service

Mike's Bikes
192 Smallwood Village Center, Waldorf
301-870-6600
No rentals

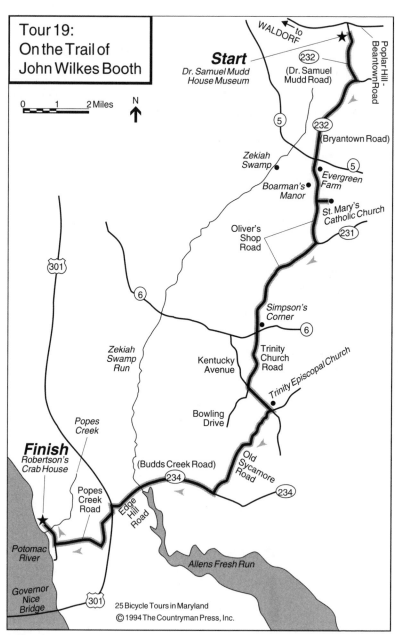

Tour 19:
On the Trail of
John Wilkes Booth

0 1 2 Miles

N

Start
Dr. Samuel Mudd
House Museum

to WALDORF

232
(Dr. Samuel
Mudd Road)

Poplar Hill -
Beantown Road

5

232

(Bryantown Road)

5

Zekiah
Swamp

Evergreen
Farm

Boarman's
Manor

St. Mary's
Catholic Church

231

Oliver's
Shop
Road

6

Simpson's
Corner

6

Zekiah
Swamp
Run

Kentucky
Avenue

Trinity
Church
Road

Trinity Episcopal Church

Bowling
Drive

301

Popes
Creek

Old
Sycamore
Road

234

Finish
Robertson's
Crab House

(Budds Creek Road)

234

Popes
Creek
Road

Edge
Hill
Road

Potomac
River

Allens Fresh Run

Governor
Nice
Bridge

301

25 Bicycle Tours in Maryland
© 1994 The Countryman Press, Inc.

19

On the Trail of John Wilkes Booth

Location: *Charles County*
Terrain: *Rolling*
Road conditions: *Paved roads with light traffic*
Distance: *23.7 miles*
Highlights: *Dr. Mudd's House, St. Mary's Church and Cemetery, Trinity Episcopal Church, Zekiah Swamp, crab restaurants on the Potomac at Pope's Creek*

Shouting "Sic semper tyrannis," John Wilkes Booth shot President Abraham Lincoln and jumped to the stage of Ford's Theater, breaking his leg. Early next morning, on his way to Confederate Virginia, he stopped at the farm of a country doctor, Samuel Mudd, who set Booth's leg. Was Mudd part of the conspiracy to kill Lincoln or just a physician following the Hippocratic oath? The guides at the restored farmhouse, some of whom are descendants of Dr. Mudd, make a strong case for the good doctor's innocence. Mudd was convicted by a military court of conspiracy in the assassination and sentenced to life imprisonment in Fort Jefferson in the Dry Tortugas. He was pardoned for his heroic service during a yellow fever epidemic, but his descendants and their supporters are trying to have the doctor exonerated and the Mudd name cleared.

This tour begins at Dr. Mudd's house, at the intersection of MD 382 and 232, west of Waldorf. After a visit to the house, which contains furniture made by Dr. Mudd in prison as well as the sofa, on which John Wilkes Booth rested, the tour visits Dr. Mudd's grave, at the church where he first met Booth, and follows a rough approximation of

Booth's escape route from Mudd's farm to the Potomac. The chief differences are that it skirts, rather than traverses, the Zekiah Swamp and that it has a happier ending: instead of crossing the Potomac and being shot in a Virginia barn, like Booth, you can end the tour eating crabs at Pope's Creek, near where Booth was ferried across the river.

0.0 *Leave Dr. Mudd's house and turn right at the end of the drive onto MD 232 (called Dr. Mudd Road at this point and then becoming Bryantown Road).*

1.7 *After climbing a small hill, Bryantown Road bears right at the fork, traversing fields of corn, soybeans, and tobacco.*

4.6 *After crossing MD 5, a four-lane highway, MD 232 becomes Olivers Shop Road.*

4.7 *Evergreen Farm, to your left, was built c. 1871.*

4.9 *To your right stands Boarman's Manor, constructed between 1674 and 1912 and part of an original tract of 3,333 acres granted in 1674 to William Boarman by Lord Baltimore.*

5.9 *Turn left into St. Mary's Catholic Church, a red-brick structure that replaced an earlier Jesuit chapel.*

Built in 1848, the church was relatively new when Samuel Mudd, a Roman Catholic, met John Wilkes Booth here after Mass, brought him home to Sunday dinner, and sold him a horse. The two later met in Washington, over drinks, when Dr. Mudd went to the city to buy Christmas presents. Still, Mudd and his wife denied recognizing Booth when he came to the house after shooting Lincoln, because Booth was disguised with stage makeup. They also claimed not to know of the assassination until after Booth had left their home, on horseback. Booth's fellow conspirator had tried to rent a carriage to make the journey easier, but Mudd's neighbors, most of them devout Catholics and parishioners of St. Mary's, refused because they needed their carriages to get to church the next day, Easter Sunday. Dr. Mudd, who died in 1883, lies buried here, shaded by cedars and oaks and surrounded by many other Mudds.

6.3 *Exit the church grounds and turn left on Olivers Shop Road.*

11.0 *Simpson's Corner, to your left, has cold drinks, snacks, and a rest room. Just past the store, Olivers Shop Road crosses MD 6 and becomes Trinity Church Road.*

12.7 *At the intersection of Bowling Drive and Kentucky Avenue, bear left, continuing on Trinity Church Road.*

13.1 *The road crosses Gilbert Swamp Run, then climbs a hill.*

13.6 *To your left is Trinity Episcopal Church.*

Trinity's Flemish bond brick walls were erected in 1793. Later, the walls were added to in order to make room for pointed-arch windows. The churchyard contains graves of Revolutionary War soldiers. Just across Trinity Church Road from the church, turn right on Old Sycamore Road, which winds past several fine examples of Maryland tobacco barns, with slats that open to let in air to dry the tobacco.

16.8 *Turn right on Budd's Creek Road, which is sometimes busy and which has a shoulder.*

19.0 *The road crosses Allen's Fresh.*

Allen's Fresh carries the waters of Zekiah Swamp to the Potomac, cutting a meandering course through marshland that shelters herons and osprey and is adorned with marsh mallow, a white flower related to the hibiscus.

20.3 *After climbing a winding hill, Budd's Creek Road ends at US 301. Cross the highway at the light and turn left, riding in the shoulder of US 301.*

20.7 *Turn right on Edge Hill Road, which winds through woods and*

A docent welcomes visitors to the home of Dr. Samuel Mudd, who set the broken leg of President Lincoln's assassin, John Wilkes Booth.

past farmhouses.

21.6 Turn right on Pope's Creek Road, passing large tobacco farms.

23.1 The road curves to the right, runs through woods, and emerges at the point where Pope's Creek runs into the wide Potomac River.

23.7 Robertson's Crab House (left) is one of three Pope's Creek restaurants specializing in hard crabs, served with a dipping sauce of vinegar and Old Bay seasoning.

Long before the Europeans came to Maryland, Indians gathered here to eat oysters, heaping the shells in piles as high as 15 feet. From the restaurants, or from the Potomac shore, look south to the Governor Nice Bridge across the Potomac—which, of course, wasn't there when John Wilkes Booth needed to get to the other side.

Bicycle Repair Service

Mike's Bikes
Pinefield Shopping
US 301 and Mattawoman-Beantown Road, Waldorf
301-870-6600
No rentals

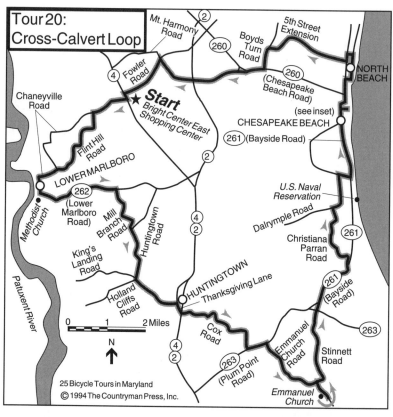

Tour 20:
Cross-Calvert Loop

Mt. Harmony Road

(2)

(260)

Boyds Turn Road

5th Street Extension

(4)

Fowler Road

(260) (Chesapeake Beach Road)

NORTH BEACH

Chaneyville Road

★ Start
Bright Center East Shopping Center

(see inset)
CHESAPEAKE BEACH

(261) (Bayside Road)

Flint Hill Road

LOWER MARLBORO

(2)

U.S. Naval Reservation

Methodist Church

(262) (Lower Marlboro Road)

Mill Branch Road

Huntingtown Road

(4) (2)

Dalrymple Road

(261)

Christiana Parran Road

King's Landing Road

Patuxent River

Holland Cliffs Road

HUNTINGTOWN — Thanksgiving Lane

(261) (Bayside Road)

(263)

0 1 2 Miles

N

(4) (2)

Cox Road

(263) (Plum Point Road)

Emmanuel Church Road

Stinnett Road

25 Bicycle Tours in Maryland
© 1994 The Countryman Press, Inc.

Emmanuel Church

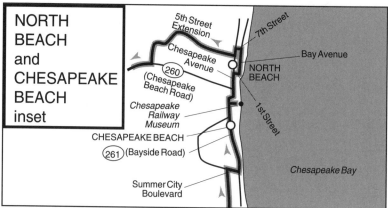

NORTH BEACH and CHESAPEAKE BEACH inset

5th Street Extension

7th Street

Chesapeake Avenue

Bay Avenue

(260) (Chesapeake Beach Road)

NORTH BEACH

Chesapeake Railway Museum

1st Street

CHESAPEAKE BEACH

(261) (Bayside Road)

Chesapeake Bay

Summer City Boulevard

142

20
Cross–Calvert Loop

Location: *Calvert County*
Terrain: *Hilly*
Road conditions: *Paved roads with light to moderate traffic*
Distance: *33.6 miles*
Highlights: *Historic Lower Marlboro, the Chesapeake Beach Railway Museum, North Beach*

Calvert County, named for Maryland's founding family, is a peninsula bounded by the Patuxent River on the west and Chesapeake Bay on the east. The rural county remains surprisingly close to the way it was when the first settlers came in the seventeenth century—although the tobacco farms that cover its rolling hills are slowly but inexorably being replaced by housing developments.

This tour begins on the ridge between the two bodies on water, on MD 4, which runs in almost a straight line from Calvert's northern border to its southern tip. After a swoop down to the Patuxent and the historic port of Lower Marlboro, the tour takes country roads back across the county and rides along the Chesapeake to the early-twentieth-century summer colonies of Chesapeake Beach and North Beach, which offer opportunities for eating and antiquing. The starting place is Bright Center East shopping center on MD 4 at Chaneyville Road, just south of the Calvert County tourist information center.

0.0 *Cross MD 4 at the light and head west on Chaneyville Road, which goes downhill, through tobacco country.*

0.9   Just past Northern High School, turn left on Flint Hill Road, which cuts through woods and farmland.

3.0   Flint Hill Road rejoins Chaneyville Road. Go straight after the stop sign.

> The eighteenth-century homes at left were moved here, by barge, from other parts of the tidewater area during the early 1970s.

3.5   Chaneyville Road curves to the left, following the shore of the Patuxent River.

> Watch for herons flying out of the marshes on the other side.

3.9   On your left, across the field, stands Patuxent River Manor.

> The Manor is an elegantly simple brick house built about 1744 by Malcolm Graham. The original paneling from the house is now at the Winterthur Museum in Delaware.

4.0   To your right is the Harbormaster's House, which serves as a reminder of the historic past of the settlement of Lower Marlboro.

> Originally called Coxtown after two early settlers, the town was renamed to honor the Duke of Marlborough after the Battle of Blenheim in 1704. By the mid-eighteenth century it was a thriving port-of-entry, with warehouses, stores, a mill, a racetrack, and many stately homes. Later the river silted up with topsoil and other ports took away the town's business. Turn right at the Harbormaster's House and follow Lower Marlboro Road down to the public dock. Until the 1930s steamboats called here to take passengers and goods to and from Baltimore.

4.1   Leave the public dock and go back up the hill to the intersection.

4.2 *Turn right on Lower Marlboro Lane for a brief tour of the village.*

A 1913 cyclone destroyed many of the old homes, and most date from the decade following that event. The white frame house at right, across the road from the Methodist churchyard, dates from about 1750, however.

4.4 *After returning to the intersection, turn right on Lower Marlboro Road (MD 262), which passes a small airport on your right and climbs a gradual hill, then descends and crosses wooded Mill Branch.*

6.7 *Turn right on Mill Branch Road, which runs through woods and tobacco fields.*

Early Marylanders used tobacco as currency, and tobacco is still an important cash crop in this area. The crop is harvested in late August and early September, and hung in barns open to the air for drying. In the winter or early spring the dried tobacco is stripped and sent to auction houses.

7.4 *At the intersection with Smoky Road, bear left on Mill Branch Road.*

8.0 *Mill Branch Road joins Huntingtown Road. Keep right on Huntingtown Road, which goes down a hill, past a small duckpond, then up a hill, through a suburban development.*

9.4 *At the intersection with Holland Cliffs Road and King's Landing Road, turn left after the stop sign and continue on Huntingtown Road.*

10.1 *At the intersection with MD 521, keep straight on Huntingtown Road (MD 521 E).*

10.6 *Turn right on Thanksgiving Lane and follow it to the blinker light at the intersection with MD 2-4. Cross the highway and continue on Cox Road, which goes through still more tobacco country.*

13.1 Cox Road ends at Plum Point Road. Turn left on Plum Point Road, which is sometimes busy but has a shoulder.

13.6 Turn right on Emmanuel Church Road, a country byway with some serious horse farms.

15.5 Emmanuel Church Road curves to the right. Follow it to its namesake, a lovely fieldstone and slate country church built between 1869 and 1901. Among the boxwoods in the churchyard are some appealing Victorian statues of angels. After visiting the church, double back on Emmanuel Church Road to the intersection with Stinnett Road.

16.4 Turn right on Stinnett Road, a hilly road through woods and residential areas.

18.5 At the intersection with MD 263 and MD 261, turn right on MD 261 N (Bayside Road), riding on the shoulder.

19.9 Turn left on Christiana Parran Road.

21.8 Christiana Parran Road ends. Turn right on Dalrymple Road, which is unmarked at this point, and follow it past a US Naval Reservation.

22.8 Turn right on Summer City Boulevard, which cuts through a vintage cottage colony.

23.2 At the stop sign, turn left on MD 261, keeping to the shoulder as it goes up and down a series of roller-coaster hills. Watch for views of the bay to your right.

25.0 Turn right on Mears Avenue.

25.1 To your right is the Chesapeake Beach Railway Museum.

> The museum is a relic of the days when the shore of Chesapeake Bay was "the beach" for people from Baltimore and Washington and when the train was the way to get there. Otto Mears, an independent short-line railroad builder from Colorado, built a grand resort here

Tobacco dries in a Calvert County barn.

in the 1890s, complete with beachfront hotels, a racetrack, a casino, bathhouses, and a boardwalk with rides and restaurants. Some people arrived by steamer, at the mile-long pier, and others took the train, called the "Honeysuckle Special," and arrived right here, at the station. The restored station houses memorabilia of the old resort and of the railway. Across the parking lot from the museum is the Rod N Reel Restaurant, which offers excellent seafood, views of the bay, and a small beach and pier. After a sojourn here, double back on Mears Avenue.

25.2 Turn right on Bayside Avenue (MD 261) and follow it through the intersection with MD 260.

26.1 Turn right on First Street, in the town of North Beach.

26.2 Turn left on Bay Avenue, which runs along the water, past the public beach and pier.

26.6 At the corner of Bay Avenue and Seventh Street stands Nice 'N Fleazy Antiques. Behind it is Elvira's Antiques. Turn left on Seventh Street, where two more antique shops are on your left in the first block.

26.7 Turn left on Chesapeake Avenue.

26.8 Turn right on Fifth Street, which goes past summer cottages built in the 1920s and earlier, and then climbs a hill and becomes the Fifth Street Extension.

29.0 Turn left on Boyds Turn Road.

29.5 Turn right on MD 260, riding on the shoulder.

29.9 At the intersection at the top of the hill, turn left on Mount Harmony Road.

31.3 Mount Harmony Road crosses MD 2 and continues.

32.3 Take a sharp left on Fowler Road, which climbs some mild hills and passes several housing developments.

33.6 Turn left into the shopping center parking lot.

Bicycle Repair Service

Penn Auto
5 Church Street (intersection of MD 4 and MD 231), Prince Frederick
410-535-2222 or 326-2864
No rentals

EASTERN
SHORE

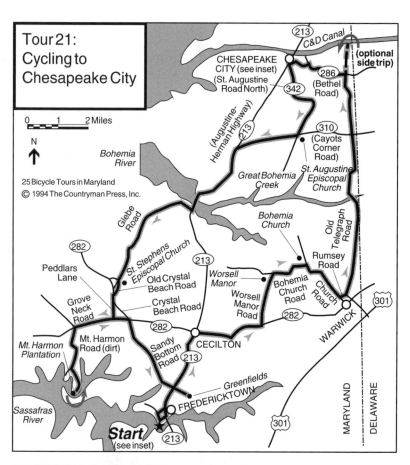

Tour 21: Cycling to Chesapeake City

0 1 2 Miles

N

25 Bicycle Tours in Maryland
© 1994 The Countryman Press, Inc.

213 C&D Canal

CHESAPEAKE CITY (see inset) (St. Augustine Road North)

(optional side trip)

342

286 (Bethel Road)

(Augustine-Herman Highway)

213

310 (Cayots Corner Road)

Bohemia River

Great Bohemia Creek

St. Augustine Episcopal Church

Bohemia Church

Glebe Road

St. Stephens Episcopal Church

282

Peddlars Lane

Old Crystal Beach Road

213

Worsell Manor

Old Telegraph Road

Rumsey Road

Grove Neck Road

Crystal Beach Road

Worsell Manor Road

Bohemia Church Road

Church Road

WARWICK

301

Mt. Harmon Plantation

Mt. Harmon Road (dirt)

282

Sandy Bottom Road

CECILTON

282

213

Sassafras River

Start (see inset)

213

Greenfields

FREDERICKTOWN

301

MARYLAND

DELAWARE

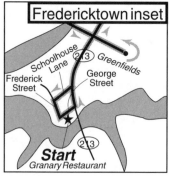

Fredericktown inset

Schoolhouse Lane

213

Greenfields

Frederick Street

George Street

Start
Granary Restaurant

213

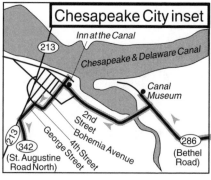

Chesapeake City inset

Inn at the Canal

213

Chesapeake & Delaware Canal

Canal Museum

2nd Street

Bohemia Avenue

4th Street

213

342 (St. Augustine Road North)

George Street

286 (Bethel Road)

21
Cycling to Chesapeake City

Location: Cecil County
Terrain: Flat to rolling
Road conditions: Mainly paved roads with light traffic
Distance: 45 miles
Highlights: Old Bohemia Church, restored Chesapeake City on the
  Chesapeake & Delaware Canal, Mount Harmon Plantation

The Chesapeake & Delaware Canal, conceived in 1661, begun in 1801, opened in 1829, and modernized in 1962, shortens the water route between Baltimore and Philadelphia by almost 300 miles. The "C&D" is also the raison d'être for the bustling, busy canal town at its western terminus, Chesapeake City, an excellent cycling destination with comfortable inns, good food, a museum, and a perfect vantage point for watching both commercial and pleasure craft sail by. Although it would certainly be feasible to complete this tour in one day, there are so many things to see on the way to Chesapeake City, as well as after arriving, that an overnight is suggested at one of the restored bed-and-breakfast inns in the historic district.

The tour begins at the Granary Restaurant in Fredericktown, a yachting center on the Sassafras River. To get there from the Washington, Baltimore, or Annapolis areas, cross the Bay Bridge and follow US 301 to the junction with MD 213, following 213 north to Georgetown and across the Sassafras River to Fredericktown. As soon as you cross the river, make the first left and follow George Street to the Granary. This is a great place to begin and/or end your journey with some Maryland crab soup or other local specialty.

0.0 Exit the parking lot, heading east along George Street, which is lined with marinas.

0.3 Cross MD 213 (Augustine Herman Highway) and turn left, riding on the shoulder up a hill.

2.0 In the midst of a field sown with soybeans stands Greenfields, a well-preserved eighteenth-century brick mansion. The house is private, but a 0.4-mile ride up the drive leads to an antique shop in the barn.

2.8 Exit the drive and continue north on MD 213.

3.8 Turn right on Main Street, MD 282, in the center of the small settlement of Cecilton.

6.0 Turn left on Worsell Manor Road.

This road is a pleasant country byway that probably looks much as it did to George Washington, who came this way in 1773 to take his stepson to Kings College (later Columbia) in New York.

7.4 On your left is Worsell Manor, the home of prominent Marylander Daniel Charles Heath; George Washington slept here.

7.6 Turn right on Bohemia Church Road.

8.8 Turn left into the church grounds.

9.0 Park your bike and explore the grounds of this beautiful brick church built about 1790 on a rise above the Little Bohemia River.

The river, the church, and many other things hereabouts derive their names from the Prague birthplace of Augustine Herman, who obtained a vast tract of land here from the Calverts in 1662 in return for making an "exact mapp" of Maryland and Virginia, a task that took ten years to complete. The real name of the church is St. Francis Xavier and it was built by Jesuits, many of whom are buried here. When Roman Catholic schools were outlawed in Maryland during the religious strife of the 1700s, a clandestine academy was established here, whose students included America's first Catholic archbishop and a signer of the Declaration of Independence, both members of the Carroll family.

The church is open the third Sunday of the month from June through September. At other times, you can admire the old boxwood, eat the wild figs growing in the yard, and pay homage at the grave of Kitty Knight, a heroine of the War of 1812. When the British tried to burn her house, she kept putting out the fire with a broom. The British finally gave up, and her house still stands in nearby Georgetown and serves as an inn.

9.2 **Exit the church grounds. Bohemia Church Road turns right here and continues as Church Road.**

10.7 **Turn right on Rumsey Road in the town of Warwick.**

This road is named for James Rumsey, born near here, who demonstrated a working steamboat on the Potomac River twenty years before Robert Fulton's better-known trial run.

10.9 **Turn left on Old Telegraph Road, a long straightaway through endearingly flat farm country.**

14.0 **Old Telegraph Road veers left to cross Great Bohemia Creek, then climbs a hill and travels through rolling countryside filled with horse farms.**

18.1 **Turn left on Bethel Road. For a preview of the C&D Canal, continue on Old Telegraph Road until it ends on a bluff with a sweeping view of the waterway. Don't try to ride on the sand road along the canal. It's hard on bikes, and the gate at the Chesapeake City end may be locked. Instead, return to Bethel Road, having added 1.8 miles to the trip.**

19.9 *Turn right on Bethel Road.*

21.1 *On your right is a museum dedicated to the history of the canal.*

There is also a pumphouse, which houses a waterwheel once used to pump water back into the canal to replace the water lost when a ship went through the lock. The modernized canal has no locks, but the Army Corps of Engineers operates out of the same building, keeping watch on canal traffic. After exiting the museum turn right on Second Street, which leads into downtown Chesapeake City.

21.6 *Turn right on Bohemia Avenue, the main street of this charmingly preserved and restored canal town.*

The Inn at the Canal is at 104 Bohemia Avenue. Across the street is the Bayard House, an excellent restaurant. The street also holds several antique shops. To leave town and start the return trip, take Bohemia Avenue away from the canal.

21.8 *Turn right on Fourth Street.*

Dead ahead of you looms the enormous bridge that overshadows Chesapeake City, high enough to let the big ships pass underneath. This one was built in 1949 after a tanker demolished one that wasn't quite tall enough.

21.9 *Turn left on George Street, which runs parallel to the bridge above.*

22.0 *Turn left on St. Augustine Road North (MD 342), which runs through race horse farm country.*

24.8 *Cross Cayots Corner Road (MD 310) and enter the grounds of St. Augustine Episcopal Church.*

The church was built in 1838 to replace an earlier structure. The large churchyard holds some Duponts and

Old Bohemia Church bears the name of the homeland of
Augustine Herman, who mapped the area in return for land.

also one Henry Craig who, at his death in 1861, requested that he be buried behind a brick wall with one brick left out so he could escape the devil. The hole has been plugged up, but the marble atop the grave is split, so maybe Craig had his way after all. After leaving the church grounds, turn left on Cayots Corner Road (MD 310).

26.7 *To your right a historical marker notes that the land hereabouts was once inhabited by the Labadists, a commune of followers of a seventeenth-century French mystic.*

27.0 *Turn left on MD 213 (Augustine Herman Highway), which has a paved shoulder.*

29.4 *After crossing the Bohemia River, turn right on Glebe Road, which runs through a small waterfront community and then turns left.*

30.2 *A general store is on the left.*

33.5 *St. Stephen's Episcopal Church, to your left, dates from 1873. At the church, turn left on Old Crystal Beach Road and continue in the same direction after this turns into Crystal Beach Road.*

33.9 *At the V go straight onto Peddler's Lane. An old blacksmith shop near the intersection sells antiques.*

34.3 *Turn right on Grove Neck Road.*

35.6 *Turn left into Mount Harmon Road.*

The road is a dirt lane, canopied by osage orange trees, that leads to Mount Harmon plantation, a Georgian manor house built in 1730 (admission fee). Watch for deer crossing the lane.

37.5 *The lane ends at the manor house, which is surrounded by boxwood gardens that lead the eye down to the Sassafras*

River, where ships called to take away tobacco grown at Mount Harmon.

39.5 After exiting the plantation grounds, turn right on Grove Neck Road.

41.0 Turn right on Sandy Bottom Road, which goes down a hill and then up another.

44.1 Turn right on MD 213 (Augustine Herman Highway).

44.7 Turn right on Schoolhouse Lane.

44.9 Turn left on Frederick Street.

45.0 Enter the parking lot of the Granary Restaurant.

Bicycle Repair Service

Bikework
208 South Cross Street, Chestertown
410-778-6940
No rentals

Accommodations

Inn at the Canal
104 Bohemia Avenue, Chesapeake City, MD 21915
410-885-5995

22
Inn to Inn on the Lower Shore

Location: Worcester County
Terrain: Flat
Road conditions: Paved roads with light traffic, paved trail on Assateague Island
Distance: 94.9 miles
Highlights: Historic Snow Hill, Chincoteague Bay, Berlin, the wild ponies of Assateague Island, the Nassawango Iron Furnace and Furnace Town, Milburn Landing State Park on the Pocomoke River

The lower Eastern Shore of Maryland is a cyclist's dream: it's almost totally flat. It also has great scenery, much preserved history, and bicycle-friendly inns. Some of these hotels and bed-and-breakfasts have joined together to provide special services to cyclists. For a per-person daily fee you get accommodations, breakfast, dinner, transport of your luggage to the next member inn, and a map for a self-guided tour. Or you can arrange your own tour and carry your own luggage.

This tour begins at the River House Inn in Snow Hill, swoops down to the Public Landing on Chincoteague Bay, leads through chicken-farm country to historic Berlin, continues to Assateague Island, where wild ponies graze on salt marsh and run by the Atlantic Ocean, and doubles back to Berlin's restored Atlantic Hotel. The second day of the tour crisscrosses the Pocomoke River and Nassawango Creek, visits an old iron furnace and restored town, and brings you back to Snow Hill.

This tour is a shorter adaptation (with the addition of a side trip to Assateague Island) of Viewtrail 100, a well-marked 100-mile tour mapped out by Worcester County.

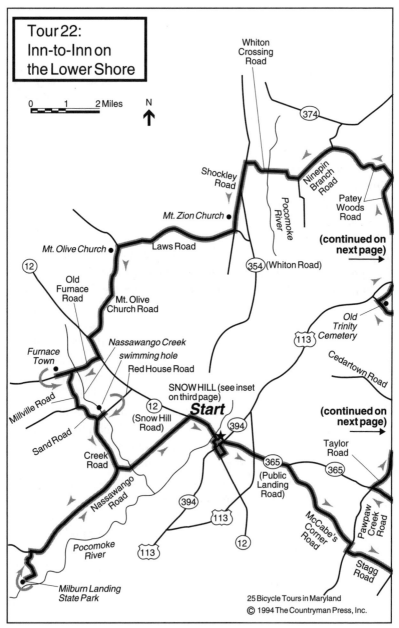

Tour 22:
Inn-to-Inn on
the Lower Shore

0   1   2 Miles   N

Whiton
Crossing
Road

374

Shockley
Road

Ninepin
Branch
Road

Patey
Woods
Road

Mt. Zion Church •

Pocomoke
River

Mt. Olive Church •   Laws Road

**(continued on
next page)**

12

354 (Whiton Road)

Old
Furnace
Road

Mt. Olive
Church Road

Old
Trinity
Cemetery

113

Cedartown Road

*Furnace
Town*

*Nassawango Creek
swimming hole*

Red House Road

SNOW HILL (see inset
on third page)

**(continued on
next page)**

Millville Road

12
(Snow Hill
Road)

Start

394

Sand Road

Taylor
Road

Creek
Road

365

365

Nassawango Road

(Public
Landing
Road)

Pawpaw Creek Road

394

113

McCabe's
Corner
Road

*Pocomoke
River*

113

12

Stagg
Road

*Milburn Landing
State Park*

25 Bicycle Tours in Maryland
© 1994 The Countryman Press, Inc.

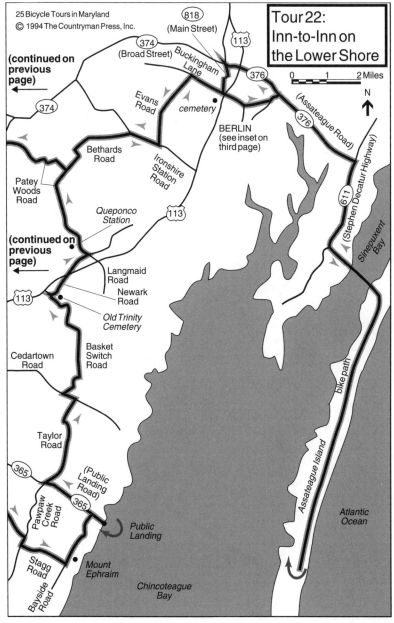

25 Bicycle Tours in Maryland
© 1994 The Countryman Press, Inc.

**Tour 22:
Inn-to-Inn on
the Lower Shore**

818
(Main Street)

374
(Broad Street)

113

Buckingham Lane

376

0   1   2 Miles

N

(continued on
previous
page)

374

Evans Road

cemetery

BERLIN
(see inset on
third page)

376

(Assateague Road)

Bethards Road

Ironshire Station Road

611

(Stephen Decatur Highway)

Sinepuxent Bay

Patey Woods Road

Queponco Station

113

(continued on
previous
page)

113

Langmaid Road

Newark Road

Old Trinity Cemetery

Cedartown Road

Basket Switch Road

bike path

Taylor Road

365

(Public Landing Road)

365

Assateague Island

Atlantic Ocean

Pawpaw Creek Road

Stagg Road

Mount Ephraim

Public Landing

Bayside Road

Chincoteague Bay

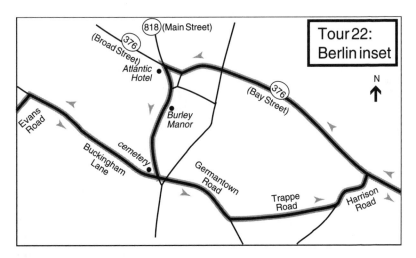

Tour 22:
Berlin inset

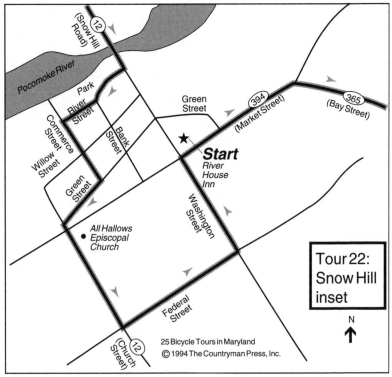

Tour 22:
Snow Hill inset

25 Bicycle Tours in Maryland
© 1994 The Countryman Press, Inc.

0.0   Leaving the River House Inn (or the adjacent municipal parking lot) turn left on Market Street (MD 394).

The River House, built c. 1860 as a Victorian country home, is set on a green lawn that rolls down to the cypress-dark Pocomoke River. Snow Hill was laid out much earlier, in 1686, and became the county seat in 1742. Since it has no hills and only rarely sees snow, it is assumed that the town was named for the English home of the original tract holder, William Stevens. The early settlers, mainly Scottish Presbyterians from Northern Ireland, wove cloth, manned grist mills, grew tobacco, and carried on commerce with England and with Barbados.

After the Revolution, Baltimore edged out Snow Hill and other colonial ports, and commerce withered. In the early nineteenth century fires devastated the old town, so much of the remaining architecture is Victorian—frame houses with lots of bric-a-brac.

0.1   Turn right on Bay Street (MD 365), which leads out of town, past a large feed mill and across railroad tracks.

1.1   Bay Street crosses US 113 and becomes Public Landing Road.

2.1   Turn right on McCabe's Corner Road, which leads through woods and past large chicken farms.

4.9   Turn right on Pawpaw Creek Road and then make an immediate left on Stagg Road.

6.3   Turn left on Bayside Road, which runs along Chincoteague Bay, source of some of the best oysters in Maryland.

This region was named "Arcadia" by Giovanni da Verrazano, who explored the area in 1524.

6.8   The yellow house at right is Mount Ephraim.

According to local lore, the inhabitants of this estate staved off a British attack by parading along the shore carrying cornstalks, which, from offshore, gave the appearance of a large military force.

8.0 **Turn right on Public Landing Road to Snow Hill Public Landing, which has a beach and a long pier with gazebos.**

The landing is a great place to sunbathe, swim, or just gaze across Chincoteague Bay, which is about five miles wide at this point. In the nineteenth century steamboats landed here and ferried people and goods to Baltimore. Just to the right of the pier is the Spence House, built in stages by a prominent local family in the 1700s and 1800s. It once served as a resort hotel known as the Mansion House.

After a respite, reverse direction and go west on Public Landing Road.

9.6 **Turn right on Taylor Road.**

12.0 **Taylor Road ends. Turn left on Cedartown Road.**

12.3 **Turn right on Basket Switch Road.**

15.8 **Turn right on Newark Road.**

15.9 **To your right, in Old Trinity Cemetery, where graves rest under tall pines, is the Bicentennial Tree.**

A historical marker, placed here in 1976, notes that the tree has stood since before the Revolution. Now, alas, it's just a stump, surrounded by poison ivy.

16.6 **Newark Road crosses US 113 and runs along railroad tracks.**

17.3 **If you need food or a rest room, turn right on Langmaid Road and proceed 0.4 mile to the convenience store/gas station on US 113 (Worcester Highway). (If you don't want to make this detour, turn left at this intersection on Patey Woods Road and deduct 0.8 mile.) After the rest stop, double back on Langmaid Road, which becomes Patey Woods Road after crossing Newark Road.**

18.1 To your left is Queponco Station, a frame nineteenth-century railroad station in the midst of restoration.

20.7 Turn right on Bethards Road, which travels through farmed fields.

23.0 Turn right on Ironshire Station Road.

23.9 Turn left on Evans Road, which is unmarked, just before the railroad crossing sign.

The deserted old house to your right is a familiar sight on the lower Eastern Shore. As farmers become more prosperous, they build modern homes and use the old ones to store crops and tools.

26.0 Turn right on Buckingham Lane.

27.2 Buckingham Lane ends at Buckingham Cemetery. Ride through the cemetery, cross Main Street, and continue in the same direction on Germantown Road, which immediately crosses US 113 (Worcester Highway).

27.8 Turn left on Trappe Road, which leads past a country church.

28.6 Turn left on Harrison Road.

28.9 Turn right on Assateague Road (MD 376). This road can be busy on summer weekends, but there is a shoulder.

31.7 Turn right on Stephen Decatur Highway (MD 611). Just after the turn, there are several camp stores where you can buy supplies for a picnic on the beach at Assateague.

35.2 The highway crosses Sinepuxent Bay on the Verrazano Bridge. The climb up this bridge is the only "hill" on the tour.

At the top, look left for a view of the skyscrapers of Ocean City. Once you cross the bridge you are on Assateague Island, which holds both a state park and a national seashore. The island's only residents are the wild ponies, descendants of horses grazed here by seventeenth-century settlers, plus white-tailed deer, Sitka deer, an Oriental elk introduced during the 1920s, and a wide variety of birds. The ponies are not ponies but horses reduced in size by inbreeding. They live in families consisting of a stallion, several mares, and their offspring. The stallion usually drives the male offspring away, and the outcasts soon start their own families. Signs warn that the ponies bite and kick, and it is illegal to feed them—they thrive on marsh and dune grass. Many of them are quite happy to pose for pictures, and can be found in the parking lots and along the roads as well as on the trails that lead to freshwater ponds in the woods. A bicycle path beside the park road leads past beautiful Atlantic beaches, a few historical exhibits, and entrances to several walking trails.

40.1 *The bike path and the road end. Travel beyond this point is either on foot or, with a permit, in a four-wheel-drive vehicle. To continue the tour double back, recross the Verrazano Bridge, and go north on MD 611.*

48.5 *Turn left on Assateague Road (MD 376), which becomes Bay Street as it enters Berlin.*

52.9 *Bay Street turns into Broad Street. Turn right on Broad Street and proceed about half a block to the Atlantic Hotel at the corner of Broad and Main.*

This restored brick commercial hotel was built in 1895 and is listed on the National Register of Historic Places. It is beautifully furnished with Victorian antiques and offers both formal dining and a pub. The Atlantic Hotel is part of the biking-from-inn-to-inn network.

To continue the trip, turn right from the front of the hotel and go south on Main Street, which is lined with Federal and Victorian homes set back from the road on well-kept lawns.

53.3 *Burley Manor, on your left, is at 313 South Main Street.*

The house was built in the early nineteenth century by descendants of the original owners of a land-grant plantation that once encompassed the whole area. The name "Berlin" is a corruption of Burley and has nothing Germanic about it.

53.7 *Bear right on the path through Buckingham Cemetery. At the end of the path, turn right on Buckingham Lane.*

54.8 *Turn left on Evans Road.*

56.9 *Evans Road dead-ends. Turn right on Ironshire Station Road.*

57.9 *At the stop sign, bear left on Bethards Road, which leads through chicken farms and cornfields into a shaded wood.*

60.1 *Turn right on Patey Woods Road.*

61.9 *At a V in front of a house, bear left on Ninepin Branch Road, which is unmarked.*

63.2 *At another V, bear right on Whiton Crossing Road.*

64.1 *Whiton Crossing Road lives up to its name by crossing the here-very-narrow Pocomoke River.*

A swimming hole on the right side of the bridge offers a refreshing dip.

"Pocomoke" means dark waters—colored by the bark of the cypresses in the swamps that feed it. Designated a "Wild and Scenic River," it is the deepest and swiftest tidal river of its width in the United States.

64.7 *Whiton Crossing Road dead ends in the small settlement of Whiton. Turn left on Whiton Road.*

65.4 *Bear right on Shockley Road.*

66.2 *The graveyard of Mount Zion Church, to your right, holds several Shockleys.*

66.7 Turn right on Laws Road, which is tree-shaded.

70.0 At Mount Olive Church, turn left on Mount Olive Church Road, which passes a radio tower and some large farms.

73.1 Turn left on Snow Hill Road (MD 12), which is sometimes busy but has a wide shoulder.

73.7 Turn right on Old Furnace Road.

74.8 To your left is Furnace Town.

Furnace Town contains the restored Nassawango Iron Furnace, Maryland's only bog furnace, and a recreated nineteenth-century town consisting of buildings moved here from other sites in the area (admission fee).

During the 1830s and 1840s, hundreds of people lived and worked on this site, gathering iron ore from nearby bogs, smelting it in the brick and stone furnace day and night, and loading the cooled pig iron onto barges to be floated down Nassawango Creek to the Pocomoke River and beyond. The creek also provided power for a saw mill and a grist mill. The surrounding town, called Nescongo, included a post office, school, church, hotel, and a mansion for the ironmaster, as well as smaller homes for the workers. By 1850, higher quality, less expensive iron was available elsewhere, and the entire town was put up for sale. There were no takers, however, and the town simply deteriorated. By the 1970s, when the county historical society took over, all that remained was the tall stack of the iron furnace.

A ramp leads visitors to the top of the stack, where the bog ore was loaded, layered between charcoal and oyster shells. The charcoal in the bottom layer was fired and hot air was forced through pipes by a bellows powered by a waterwheel. The ore melted and flowed to the bottom, with the oyster shells filtering out impurities.

Berlin's restored Atlantic Hotel provides food and lodging for cyclists.

75.0 *Just past the entrance to Furnace Town, turn left on Millville Road (unmarked), which has Nassawango Creek and a pine-and-holly woods on one side and a cornfield on the other.*

The creek side of the road is a sanctuary owned by the Nature Conservancy.

75.9 *Millville Road ends at the intersection with Sand Road. Bear left on Sand Road.*

76.6 *At the intersection with Red House Road, a slight jog to the left on Red House Road will take you to a pleasant swimming hole on Nassawango Creek. Then continue on Sand Road, which becomes Creek Road.*

78.7 *Turn right on Nassawango Road.*

82.7 *Turn left into Milburn Landing State Park and follow the signs to a landing and dock on the Pocomoke River.*

84.7 *From the landing, retrace your path on Nassawango Road to the intersection with Creek Road. Continue on Nassawango, crossing a wide expanse of lily-pad-covered creek on a bridge.*

93.0 *Turn left on Snow Hill Road (MD 12) and cross the Pocomoke into Snow Hill.*

94.2 *Immediately after crossing the bridge, turn right into a riverfront park with rest rooms and the landing of* Tillie the Tug, *an excursion boat that plies the river.*

94.3 *Turn left on Commerce Street and then right on Green Street.*

94.4 *Cross Market Street onto Church Street.*

On your right stands All Hallows Episcopal Church, built in 1756 in Flemish bond with glazed headers. There were some Victorian renovations, notably a slate roof.

94.6 *Turn left on Federal Street.*

This street is lined with gracious nineteenth-century homes. The main part of the house at 101 West Federal was built c. 1800 using ship's ballast. Later, the house may have been part of the underground railroad.

94.7 Turn left on Washington Street.

94.9 Turn right on Market Street and return to the River House Inn.

Bicycle Repair Services

A.W. Payne Western Auto
114 West Green Street, Snow Hill
410-632-1334
No rentals

Bike World
10 Caroline Street, Ocean City
410-289-2587
Rentals

Accommodations

The River House Inn
201 East Market Street, Snow Hill, MD 21863
410-632-2722

Atlantic Hotel
2 North Main Street, Berlin, MD 21811
410-641-3589

For information on Biking Inn-to-Inn on the Eastern Shore, write P.O. Box 20, Betterton, MD 21610.

WESTERN
MARYLAND

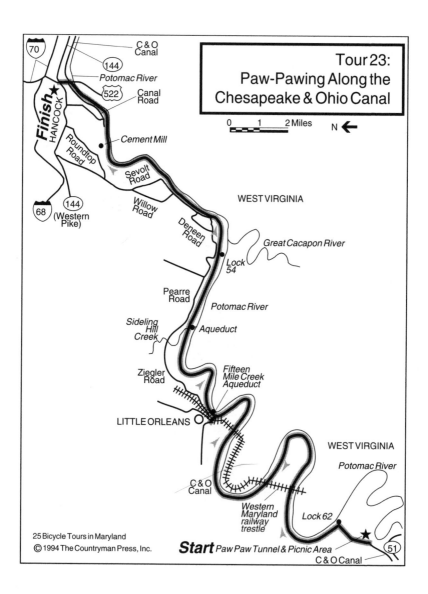

70
C & O Canal
144
Potomac River
522
Canal Road

★ **Finish** HANCOCK

Tour 23:
Paw-Pawing Along the
Chesapeake & Ohio Canal

0 1 2 Miles N ←

Roundtop Road

Cement Mill

Sevolt Road

68 **144** (Western Pike)

Willow Road

WEST VIRGINIA

Deneen Road

Lock 54

Great Cacapon River

Pearre Road

Potomac River

Sideling Hill Creek

Aqueduct

Ziegler Road

Fifteen Mile Creek Aqueduct

LITTLE ORLEANS ○

WEST VIRGINIA

Potomac River

C & O Canal

Western Maryland railway trestle

Lock 62

Lock 51

Start Paw Paw Tunnel & Picnic Area

C & O Canal

25 Bicycle Tours in Maryland
© 1994 The Countryman Press, Inc.

23
The Paw Paw Tunnel

Location: *Allegany and Washington Counties*
Terrain: *Flat*
Road conditions: *Hard-packed dirt towpath in good condition*
Distance: *32.2 miles*
Highlights: *The Paw Paw Tunnel, Little Orleans, Hancock*

To avoid digging the Chesapeake & Ohio Canal around a six-mile bend of the Potomac, the engineers decided on a 3,118-foot tunnel right through a mountain that took thousands of workers 14 years to complete. This tour begins in the picnic area adjacent to the tunnel, which is across the Potomac from Paw Paw, West Virginia on MD 51. After walking your bike through the narrow, very dark tunnel with the aid of your own flashlight, you proceed along the wooded towpath, stopping for dips in the river and refreshment at Bill's Place, a historic general store-cum-tavern just off the towpath in the village of Little Orleans. The tour ends in Hancock, a once-bustling canal town with several down-home restaurants. Unless you want to retrace your path, leave one car in Hancock on the way to Paw Paw.

0.0 **Leave the picnic area and follow the signs to the tunnel.**

The Paw Paw tunnel was built at a cost of about $600,000. Workers, many of them Irish and German immigrants, were paid $10 a month, plus a daily ration of whiskey and meat. They used black gun powder to blast through the rock and lined the resulting tunnel with five or six layers of bricks. Ethnic feuds plus a cholera epidemic slowed the work.

Cyclists emerge from the mile-long Paw Paw Tunnel,
cut through the mountains for the Chesapeake & Ohio Canal.

In canal days, the downstream boat had the right of way in the tunnel. Now, just walk slowly, use a flashlight, and be careful of other bikers and hikers.

1.1 *Emerge from the tunnel and continue on the towpath, which makes a straightaway, away from the river, through a hollow.*

2.8 *At Lock 62, which is lined with wood, the towpath begins following the Potomac River.*

5.7 *The towpath crosses under the first of several Western Maryland Railway trestles across the Potomac.*

Because the river bends sharply and often at this point and hills rise just above its banks, it apparently made sense to route the railroad tracks back and forth across the river.

15.2 *The towpath crosses Fifteen Mile Creek Aqueduct, a 110-foot stone arch completed between 1848 and 1850. Leave the towpath here and bear left, on a paved road, to the small settlement of Little Orleans.*

This old German settlement became a mini-boomtown during the building of the canal. Many Irish canal workers, some of them victims of a cholera epidemic, are buried at St. Patrick's Catholic Church on the hill above the town. Of more immediate interest is the Orleans Grocery, or Bill's Place, which functions as a camp store, pool hall, bar, and restaurant and which has an inviting porch swing. It was moved from the banks of the river to its present location in 1904 to make room for railroad tracks.

19.7 *The towpath passes over Sideling Hill Creek Aqueduct.*

22.3 *At Lock 54, look across to the West Virginia side at the point where the Great Cacapon River enters the Potomac.*

28.8 *The Roundtop Cement Mill, now a ruin, is on your left.*

The mill was built here in 1837 to turn newly discovered local limestone into cement for the canal. It closed in 1909.

32.1 Cross the canal on a bridge to Canal Street, which parallels the canal.

32.2 Turn left on Pennsylvania Avenue, which leads to Main Street in Hancock.

Bicycle Repair Service

Cycles & Things
165 North Centre Street, Cumberland
301-722-5496
No rentals

24
Deep Creek Loop

Location: *Garrett County*
Terrain: *Very hilly*
Road conditions: *Mainly paved light-traffic roads, with a one-mile stretch on a busy road and one dirt road*
Distance: *33.9 miles*
Highlights: *Deep Creek Lake, the Cranesville Sub-Arctic Swamp, Swallow Falls, Muddy Creek Falls*

The biggest freshwater lake in Maryland, 3,900-acre Deep Creek Lake was created in the 1920s as part of a hydroelectric project. Even before the lake became a recreation Mecca, the surrounding area drew outdoors aficionados. In 1918, Henry Ford, Harvey Firestone, and Thomas Edison camped at Muddy Creek Falls. Even earlier Grover Cleveland, a more sedentary type, honeymooned in nearby Deer Park.

This tour, which is decidedly not for sedentary types, begins in Deep Creek Lake State Park, where you can have a swim before or after the ride. It skirts the lake for a bit, then runs alongside Sang Run and the Youghiogheny River and makes its way over a mountain road to the Cranesville Sub-Arctic Swamp, a nature sanctuary. After stops at two spectacular waterfalls, the tour returns to Deep Creek Lake State Park.

0.0   *Exiting the park, turn left on State Park Road, which leads across a bridge.*

0.3   *As soon as you cross the bridge, turn right on Glendale Road, which crosses another bridge.*

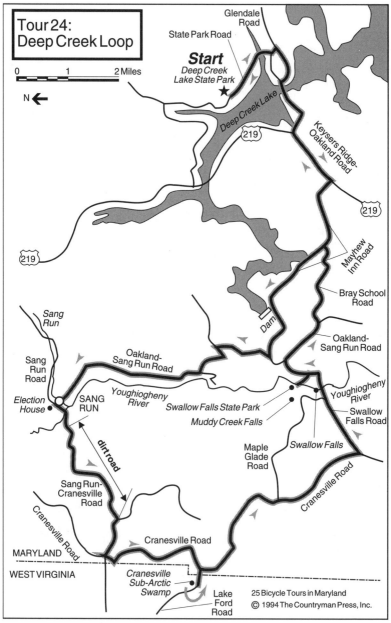

**Tour 24:
Deep Creek Loop**

0   1   2 Miles

N ←

Glendale Road

State Park Road

Start
*Deep Creek
Lake State Park* ★

Deep Creek Lake

219

Keysers Ridge-
Oakland Road

219

Mayhew Inn Road

Bray School Road

219

Dam

Oakland-
Sang Run Road

Sang Run

Sang Run Road

Election House ●

SANG RUN

Youghiogheny River

● Swallow Falls State Park
● Muddy Creek Falls

Youghiogheny River

Swallow Falls Road

dirt road

Swallow Falls

Maple Glade Road

Cranesville Road

Sang Run-
Cranesville Road

Cranesville Road

Cranesville Road

MARYLAND

WEST VIRGINIA

*Cranesville
Sub-Arctic
Swamp* ●

Lake Ford Road

25 Bicycle Tours in Maryland
© 1994 The Countryman Press, Inc.

Although it's only 12 miles in length, Deep Creek Lake has a shoreline of 65 miles. Its waters seem to flow into all the nooks and crannies of the land. As a result, riding along the lake means crossing many bridges over narrow sections of water.

2.3   *Turn left on US 219 (Oakland Road), which can be busy but has a shoulder.*

3.3   *Turn right on Mayhew Inn Road, which has a restaurant on the corner.*

4.0   *The stone barn at your right is in the style characteristic of the area.*

6.4   *To your right is the dam that created the lake.*

7.6   *Turn right on Oakland-Sang Run Road, which runs up and down hills covered with hemlocks, laurel, and rhododendron.*

The Youghiogheny River—affectionately known by river rafters as "the Yuck"—can be heard, more often than seen, on your left.

12.9 *Turn left on Sang Run Road, in the small settlement of Sang Run, after stopping for refreshment in Friends Store at the intersection.*

"Sang" is short for ginseng, a medicinal plant prized in Asia as an aphrodisiac. The wild plant once grew in profusion hereabouts and provided income for local farmers.

13.0 *The Election House to your right served as a polling place from 1882 to 1972. Across the road, a park on Sang Run offers picnic tables.*

13.3 *Sang Run Road crosses the Youghiogheny River, passes a farmhouse, bears left, turns to hard-packed dirt, and begins climbing Piney Mountain, following the river on a high ridge.*

To your right, breaks in the forest afford sweeping mountain views.

15.9 Turn left on Cranesville Road. Ignore the misleading signs to the Cranesville Sub-Arctic Swamp and continue south on Cranesville Road, up a winding hill and past several farms.

18.1 Just past a small white church, turn right on Lake Ford Road, which turns to dirt-and-gravel and leads across the West Virginia line to the swamp, which is owned by the Nature Conservancy.

Secure your bike in the parking lot and follow signs to the boardwalk built over the swamp, a remnant of the Ice Age. Some plants found in this bog normally grow only in Arctic climes.

18.8 Exiting the preserve, turn right, continuing south on Cranesville Road.

23.1 Make a sharp left onto Swallow Falls Road.

24.4 Turn left into Swallow Falls State Park.

Secure your bike and take a short hike from the parking lot to Swallow Falls and Muddy Creek Falls. Muddy Creek Falls, at 51 feet, is the highest waterfall in Maryland. Henry Ford, Harvey Firestone, and Thomas Edison camped here in 1918 and again in 1921. A photograph now in the Ford Museum in Dearborn, Michigan, shows the pioneer automaker scrubbing his laundry in the creek. Just downstream, Muddy Creek empties into the Youghiogheny River, which quickly tumbles down Swallow Falls, named for the birds that nest in the crevices the river has made in the rocks.

25.3 Exiting the park, turn left on Swallow Falls Road.

25.7 After passing a camp store to your left, Swallow Falls Road winds uphill, lined by tall pines.

26.6 Turn right on Oakland-Sang Run Road.

27.5 Turn left on Bray School Road.

A boardwalk leads through the Cranesville Sub-Arctic Swamp,
a relic of an earlier, colder age.

29.2 *Turn right on Mayhew Inn Road.*

30.6 *Turn left on US 219.*

31.6 *Turn right on Glendale Road and follow it across the bridge.*

32.8 *Turn left on State Park Road.*

33.9 *Return to Deep Creek Lake State Park.*

Bicycle Repair Services

High Mountain Sports
Route 219, McHenry
301-387-4199
Rentals

Rudy's
Wisp Resort, McHenry
301-387-4640
Rentals

Accommodations:

Garrett County Promotion Council
200 Third Street, Oakland, MD 21550
301-334-1948

25
New Germany

Location: *Garrett County*
Terrain: *Very hilly*
Road conditions: *Paved country roads*
Distance: *15.5 miles*
Highlights: *New Germany State Park, the National Road, Casselman River Bridge, Penn Alps Restaurant, and artisans' village.*

Garrett County played an important part in America's westward push. General Braddock pioneered a military road through here en route to Fort Duquesne—now Pittsburgh—during the French and Indian War. The National Pike—now Alternate US 40—followed. Today, Garrett County's roads are fine for biking, if you don't mind a few hills. Named for John Garrett, a Baltimore & Ohio Railroad official who promoted the area as "America's Switzerland," this is Maryland's highest and westernmost county. Its forested Allegheny Mountain slopes are home to both game and skiers, and its rivers beckon fisherman and kayakers.

This tour begins in New Germany State Park, journeys along the National Pike across the Casselman River Bridge into Grantsville, and then follows the Casselman River south, looping back to the park.

0.0 *Exit the state park, which has a swimming lake, boat rental, cabins, campsites, and hiking trails, and head north on New Germany Road. The road cuts through farm country and rolls up and down hills.*

5.1 *After passing over US 40/I-68, turn left on Alt. US 40, the National Pike.*

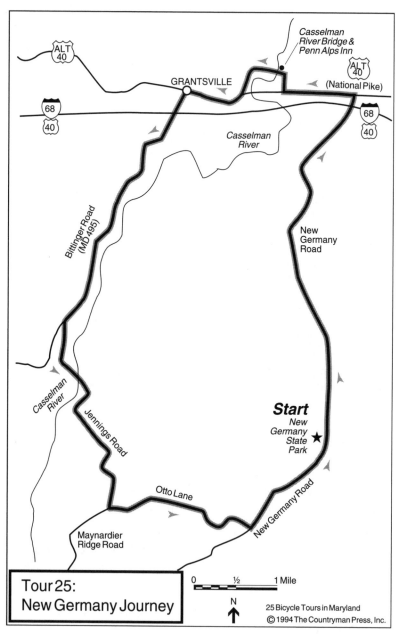

ALT 40

GRANTSVILLE

Casselman
River Bridge &
Penn Alps Inn

ALT 40
(National Pike)

68
40

68
40

Casselman
River

Bittinger Road
(MD 495)

New
Germany
Road

Casselman
River

Jennings Road

Start
New
Germany
State
Park

Otto Lane

New Germany Road

Maynardier
Ridge Road

**Tour 25:
New Germany Journey**

0   ½   1 Mile

N

25 Bicycle Tours in Maryland
© 1994 The Countryman Press, Inc.

In the early 1800s, the infant federal government began an ambitious road-building program. The National Road, which roughly followed General Braddock's route, was built as an extension of the Cumberland Road, and ran from Cumberland to the Ohio River. Now Alt. US 40, the road carries mainly local traffic, and there is a shoulder.

6.3 *An old mile marker for the National Road stands at right.*

6.7 *Bear right at the bottom of the hill to the Casselman River Bridge, which is closed to automobile traffic.*

This single-arch stone bridge, originally constructed in 1813–1814 as part of the National Road and restored in 1911, is now part of Casselman River State Park. A steel bridge, built in 1933, carries Alt. US 40 traffic. George Washington crossed the river at this point, known as Little Crossings, while serving as a military aide to General Braddock. When it was constructed, the 89-foot stone span was the largest of its type in America. Reportedly, it was constructed a little longer than necessary in the hope that the planned Chesapeake & Ohio Canal would pass under it, but the canal went only as far west as Cumberland. At the opening ceremony for the bridge many expressed surprise when the supporting timbers were removed and the bridge did not collapse. The Penn Alps Inn, built adjacent to the bridge in 1818 to serve stagecoach passengers, is still serving food and drink. Next to the inn are reconstructed log houses and a minivillage where craftspeople demonstrate their skills and sell their wares. After crossing the stone bridge, bear left and continue west on Alt. US 40.

7.6 *In the center of Grantsville, turn left on Bittinger Road (MD 495), which leads down a long hill and along the Casselman River, to your left.*

10.0 *Bittinger Road crosses the Casselman River and then climbs a*

hill.

11.0 *Turn left on Jennings Road, which passes a stone church, crosses a creek, and winds up a long hill.*

13.6 *Turn left on Maynardier Ridge Road, which winds down a long hill with excellent valley views and becomes Otto Lane.*

14.9 *Turn left on New Germany Road.*

15.5 *Re-enter New Germany State Park.*

Bicycle Repair Services

High Mountain Sports
Route 219, McHenry
301-387-4199
Rentals

Allegany Bike Works
14419 National Highway, LaVale
301-729-9708
Rentals

Accommodations

The Casselman Motor Inn
Main Street, Grantsville, MD 21536
301-895-5055

Cabins and Campsites

New Germany State Park
Route 2, Grantsville, MD 21536
301-895-5453

More Biking Guides from Backcountry Publications

Backcountry Publications is well known for its books on biking, hiking, walking, fishing, and other outdoor recreational activities. Here's a sample of what we have to offer.

Biking

30 Bicycle Tours in Wisconsin:
 Lakes, Forests, and Glacier-Carved Countryside
25 Bicycle Tours in Maine: Coastal & Inland Rides from Kittery to Caribou
25 Mountain Bike Tours in Massachusetts:
 From the Connecticut River to the Atlantic Coast
25 Mountain Bike Tours in Vermont:
 Scenic Tours Along Dirt Roads, Forest Trails, and Forgotten Byways
30 Bicycle Tours in New Hampshire:
 A Guide to Selected Backcountry Roads throughout the Granite State
25 Bicycle Tours in Vermont:
25 Bicycle Tours in the Hudson Valley:
 Scenic Rides from Saratoga to West Point
25 Bicycle Tours on Delmarva:
 Day Trips and Overnights on the Eastern Shore of the Chesapeake Bay
25 Bicycle Tours in Eastern Pennsylvania:
 Day Trips and Overnights from Philadelphia to the Highlands
25 Bicycle Tours in New Jersey:
 Over 900 Miles of Scenic Pleasures and Historic Treasures
25 Bicycle Tours in and around Washington, D.C.
25 Bicycle Tours in Ohio's Western Reserve: Historic Northeast Ohio
 from the Lake Erie Islands to the Pennsylvania Border

We offer many more books on hiking, travel, biking, walking, fishing, and canoeing in the Midwest, New England, New York, and the Mid-Atlantic states—plus our mysteries, history, gardening, and how-to.

Our books are available at bookstores, or they may be ordered directly from the publisher. For ordering information or for a complete catalog, please contact:

The Countryman Press
c/o W.W. Norton & Company, Inc.
800 Keystone Industrial Park
Scranton, PA 18512
http://web.wwnorton.com